Praise for author Stephen Kiesling
and
The Shell Game

An examination of athletics as a metaphor for the strivings of the human spirit . . . **the most exciting sports narrative I've read.**

—*The Wall Street Journal*

Just as it is good that there was one serious riverboat pilot who could write . . . it is good that there is one true blue jock who can.

—*The New York Times Book Review*

Kiesling's writing pulses . . . Brims with humor, poetic description and a strong penchant for storytelling.

—*The Evening Post*, Charleston, SC

Nicely crafted . . .

—*The Washington Post Sunday Book World*

His sense of humor never falters . . .

—*Arkansas Gazette*

I liked its sharp, lively writing. It's a good exposition of the European, dualistic, competitive approach to Quality, which is so different from the monistic, immersive approach found in *Zen and the Art of Archery* . . . I hope the book does well.

—Robert M. Pirsig,
Author of *Zen and the Art of Motorcycle Maintenance*

It is a gem . . .

—*The Baltimore Sun*

WALKING THE
PLANK

A True Adventure Among Pirates

STEPHEN KIESLING

Nordic Knight Press
Ashland, Oregon

Copyright © 1994 by Stephen Kiesling

Printed in the United States of America

First Printing

1 2 3 4 5 6 7 8 9

Library of Congress Cataloging-in-Publication Data

Kiesling, Stephen.
Walking the plank : a true adventure among pirates / Stephen Kiesling
        p.   cm.
    ISBN 0-9638461-5-9 : $12.95
    1. Whidah (ship) 2. Shipwrecks—Massachusetts—Cape Cod. 3. Stockbrokers—United States—Corrupt practices. I. Title.
G530.W5787K54 1994
974.4 ' 92--dc20

                                        94-7436
                                        CIP

In memory of

**Timothy Egan Lenahan,
Architect**

July 1, 1958—September 7, 1992

*Who took my hand
and told me to tell the truth.*

John F. Kennedy, Jr.: Taking a break from Brown University, the president's son spent the summer of 1983 working just off Cape Cod as first mate aboard Barry Clifford's salvage boat, *Vast Explorer II*.

(photo by Karen Jeffrey, *Cape Cod Times*)

I take it, no fool ever made a bargain for his soul
with the devil:
the fool is too much of a fool or the devil too
much of a devil—
I don't know which.

—Joseph Conrad, Heart of Darkness

Prologue

I was on assignment for a travel magazine, drinking my way through the Parisian haunts of Ernest Hemingway, when I heard glass shatter in the *Place St. Germain des Pres,* across the street from my perch at the *Cafe aux Deux Magots.* More glass shattered, then more, until it sounded like a story. I needed one of those, a real one, so I signaled for the check.

To my way of thinking, the Parisian junket was not really dishonorable. True, A*ir France* gave me a free airplane ticket and hoped that I would write something nice about them, but they would be happy with any article about Paris whether I mentioned them or not. My only hesitation was the story, an impossible cliché. But it was August. Vacation funds were low. And Paris! Perhaps even on this worn path, the ghost of Hemingway might speak to me. In any case, Papa would have appreciated the trip: it was the first time in my new career as a freelance writer that a magazine had agreed in advance to pick up my bar tab.

I settled my account and ambled across the street where a small crowd had gathered around the source of the noise. At six-feet, five-inches tall, I could stand in the back and watch the wiry, muscular man who squatted under the street light. He was about my own age, thirty, with a rough, pock-marked face. Beside him was a cardboard box filled with old wine bottles. In front of him a second box yawned empty. He was systematically removing the bottles from the first box, two at a time, and then smashing them together so the shards fell into the second. No one knew why, and he paid no attention to us until he was done. He swirled the shards around inside the box and dumped them out on the flagstones in a neat circle that was roughly two feet in diameter and eight inches high. The pile gleamed scarlet in the headlights of passing cars.

The fellow scanned the crowd, pointed my way, and demanded to know how much I weighed.

"Cent kilos," I called back. Two hundred and twenty pounds.

This pleased him, and he motioned for me and one other large fellow to join him under the light. I had no idea what he was going to do, and, therefore, did not back out. He positioned the two of us facing each other on either side of the pile and had us grasp each other's wrists to form a bridge. Then he hunkered down before the pile like a man warming himself at a fire. He placed his palms on the ground, and thrust his legs out behind him as if to do a push-up with his face over the broken glass.

He flexed his arms. His nose hit the glass with a soft crunch like gravel underfoot. He took his hands from the ground so that his full weight was supported between the toes of his sneakers on the flagstones and his face in the pile of glass. Then he began to tug on my ankle. He wanted my foot on the back of his neck.

I placed the ball of my loafer as gently as possible onto the back of his neck. Then he grasped my left leg and began to tug once more. He wanted both feet, all two hundred and twenty pounds, on the back of his neck. The crowd was quiet. I could not read a single expression. Even the face of the stranger whose wrists I held (for balance, I now understood) was blank. Ever so slowly I shifted my weight off the flagstones. I could hear the shards break. I could feel the man's face ratchet downward. When all of my weight was on his neck, he took his hands from my ankles and turned his thumbs up toward the crowd, who cheered.

I exhaled sharply, in relief, and the pile settled again. The sound was different. Squishy. I stepped off.

He looked as if he had fallen from some great height and landed face first, splattering himself on the flagstones. I just stared, transfixed, until he put his hands on the ground and began to press up. His face was a mask of burgundy, which turned out to be glass fragments clinging to his skin. He was unscratched.

He raced around collecting coins and bills while I gathered my wits. I didn't know whether to be impressed or angry or ashamed.

"Why me?" I asked finally.

"Cent kilos," he said. "You have an honest face." He turned away.

I wondered what Papa would have done if his feet were on the neck of a man who buried his face in a pile of glass, but I never wrote the story because the magazine lost its financing while I was in Paris. I got stuck with the bar tab, and the episode became a tiny sore on the edge of my memory. It would take me years to sort out what that Frenchman told me. You look like a sucker, he had said. A very big one.

I, for what I have heard with my own ears, and my farflung informants found it difficult to remember exactly what people said back when the war was starting up or in the thick of it. Thus, I have put down what I thought was most appropriate for them to say in the given situation, while keeping as close as I could to the overall sense of what was actually said.

—Thucydides, circa 410 B.C.
translated by J.B. Kiesling

Walking the Plank is based on incomplete notes and recollections. Conversations have been condensed and in some cases recreated. Two names haven been changed. And so, while I cannot claim that this is a true account of what happened, I do claim that it is honest.

Coming Aboard

Nothing remarkable was ever accomplished in a prosaic mood. The heroes and discoverers have found that true more than was previously believed, only when they were expecting and dreaming of something more than their contemporaries dreamed of, or even themselves discovered, that is, when they were in a frame of mind fitted to behold the truth. Referred to the world's standard, they are always insane.

—Henry David Thoreau,
Cape Cod, circa 1850

The treasure hunter Barry Clifford swaggered into the book packager's offices wearing a blue blazer, turquoise polo shirt, corduroy trousers, penny loafers without socks, and a tan *Expedition Whydah* baseball cap, which he did not remove. He was forty-five, about five feet ten. Bull necked. Barrel chested. His shoulders threatened to burst through his blazer. A plug of muscle, Clifford might have looked menacing except for the cap and the white blob of spit that hung in the corner of his mouth. It was almost as big as a piece of gum. In his left hand he brandished a rolled-up copy of the day's *The New York Times*.

"We got knocked off the front page!" was the first thing he said, smacking the newspaper against his thigh. His voice had a Massachusetts slur. The white blob stretched and bubbled when he spoke. "Those idiots leaked the story to *USA Today*." Then he smiled, a dazzling white smile that made his Irish blue eyes light up. He held out his right hand and appeared genuinely glad to meet me. I don't like salesmen much, but this guy was so transparent it was hard to dislike him. My reservations about being there faded a little.

I had arrived at the book packager's office on time, some twenty minutes earlier. That day, June 28, 1989, was a few days into a record-setting heat wave, and the air hung thick and sooty over Manhattan's Flatiron District, the low-rent hotbed of publishing startups. At 6 West 20th Street, the cracked, grime-colored marble lobby was as hot as a pizza oven, and the single elevator was of the slow, grinding sort that appears in suspense movies. On the eleventh floor, the top, the elevator door rattled open into a dim foyer. The right wall had a small reception window into the offices beyond. I pressed the buzzer, and a woman in her mid-twenties with close-cropped hair appeared in the window. A louder buzzer sounded, and I pushed through an Arctic blast into the offices of the Phillip Lief Group. Instantly, my glasses fogged, and I was fumbling. I regretted for a moment not having worn contact lenses, but the cold air made me much more comfortable in my tweed jacket with the leather elbow patches.

I looked ridiculous—just like a philosophy major and

freelance writer ought to.

The space was long and narrow and white. A fashionably rustic and uninviting sofa was in tripping distance against the left wall. To the right, over a chest-high partition and across a hallway, three small offices faced the street. Paned-glass walls and doors revealed a young woman busy in each.

The boss, Phillip Lief, was behind the closed wooden door at the far end. Judging from the book jackets framed along the walls Lief was in the cookbook and self-help business: standard fare for packagers, because real publishers don't want the hassle. Yet there was also an adventure novel written by a fighter pilot. Perhaps this new book about Barry Clifford and the pirate ship *Whydah* was Lief's leap into serious nonfiction.

A step anyway.

The treasure hunter still held the rolled-up newspaper grandly, like a sword: "My idea of a home run in this business is to be on the front page of *The New York Times*," he was saying. He was waiting for me to reach for the paper, and I would have let him wait. But if I didn't reach for it, I would have kept staring at the white blob of spit. I reached, and Clifford passed it over as if he'd won something.

I flipped to page A-14 and read:

Salvagers Find Hulk of Galleon South of Florida:
Historians See Porthole to Past in Old Vessel

Tampa, Fla., June 27 — In what archaeologists say may be one of the most important discoveries ever of a Spanish galleon, a ship from the early 1600's has been found off southwest Florida in 1,500 feet of water, a depth where the temperature and pressure have apparently preserved much of the wooden vessel and her cargo.

7

The *Times* attributed the discovery of the galleon to a salvage company called Seahawk, which had "established an association with two of the leading salvagers of colonial wrecks, Robert F. Marx and Barry Clifford."

"We are going to take over the treasure industry," Clifford announced, still grinning.

Before that moment I hadn't thought of treasure hunting as an industry; but if it were, Clifford hardly appeared the sort who could take it over. It was easy to picture him in his first occupations: raising money for the Boy Scouts and teaching high school PE. I could envision him outside a suburban front door wearing blue shorts, knee socks, and a beanie cap. I would have given him money because he was so earnest and because he would then go away. I could also picture him as an assistant football coach, the guy who's trying to act as tough as the old head coach and still wants everybody to like him. It was hard to see Clifford in his next job, a real estate developer. Harder still to see him taking over an industry.

And yet he was.

The woman with close-cropped hair ushered Clifford and me through the wooden door into Phillip Lief's office. It was the corner office, the largest by far. Through the plate-glass windows, the last of the morning sun streamed down to the wood floors. Back-lit, with his face in shadow, Phillip Lief stood beside his chair talking fast like a lawyer into a speaker phone. He was a sharp-featured wisp of a man wearing a crisp European-cut business suit and gleaming black shoes. He could have been lost for days behind his massive wooden desk.

Lief clicked off the phone, stepped forward, and clapped Clifford on the shoulder. He shook hands with me.

"That was a great piece you did in *The New Yorker*," Lief said. "Not many writers have published in both *Sports Illus-*

trated and *The New Yorker*—not to mention getting your first book reviewed in the *Times.*" This was for Clifford's benefit. For no particular reason, I doubted Lief had read the stuff I sent him. Lief looked toward Clifford: "Steve was on the Olympic team."

"What sport?" The treasure hunter asked.

"Rowing."

"When?"

"1980. Moscow." I winced at the second part. It always felt like saying I was a passenger aboard the *Titanic.*

Clifford winced sympathetically. "What a shame. I guess it was like Viet Nam. More noble not to go, but you wonder."

I hadn't thought about it that way.

"You try out in '84?" Lief asked, just being polite.

"Yeah, sort of. I was fitness editor of *American Health* magazine and had a crazy plan to make the Olympic team training only an hour a day. We survived to the finals. Then we crashed and burned."

"Where'd you go to college?" Clifford asked.

"Yale."

The treasure hunter smiled as if I had said something funny. Odd for a guy who had gone somewhere in Colorado that no one had ever heard of.

Lief gestured to a sofa and chairs around a coffee table. I took the sofa, and Lief and Clifford took the chairs. As we sat down, the woman with the close-cropped hair appeared with a coffeepot. She was prepared to serve, but Lief took the pot and sent her away. Cups were on the table, and he poured my coffee—an act that did not come naturally.

I knew that Lief had signed a contract with Clifford to package the pirate book. Clifford's job was to provide the story and do the talk-show circuit. Lief's job was to find an author to write the manuscript, an editor to clean it up, and a publisher to advance funds for the project and print the books. My job—if Clifford liked me, and I wanted it—was to write the book. I would produce the manuscript but would have no rights to it. My credit, if there were any, would be "written with." I would be the fifth wheel on which the entire project rolled forward. Still, I couldn't turn down the book without hearing the details. My next assignment from *Sports Illustrated* was a couple of weeks away, and this meeting would finish with a free lunch.

I got out a pen and one of those speckled composition books favored by school kids and started to take notes.

Meanwhile, the packager had inserted a videotape into a VCR built into a wall cabinet. He fast-forwarded the tape to a montage of sights and sounds of Barry Clifford's salvage operation. A helicopter shot of a salvage vessel was followed by a scuba diver's view of pirate cannons half-buried in sand. The next cut was to the face of an unidentified seaman wearing a blue baseball cap and gazing out over a flat ocean. He wasn't old; maybe early thirties, but he had the tone of the Ancient Mariner. "A lot of people think we're just here to pull up the treasure and get rich," the seaman said. "But we're here to learn about history and to teach the rest of the world about a history nobody knows about."

Then came another voice. Unmistakeable. Jarring. I looked again at Clifford, who grinned, suddenly bashful.

"What's this?" My voice sounded more incredulous than I intended.

"A CBS News special," he answered. *"Walter Cronkite at Large."*

I didn't want to hear about the pirate wreck from Cronkite. I wanted to hear the story directly from Clifford and make my own decision. But there was no ignoring that voice. One of my first memories was Cronkite, in shirtsleeves, saying that President Kennedy was dead. I grew up on reruns of *You Are There* with Cronkite interviewing heroes like Paul Revere and Thomas Edison.

From Edison to Clifford. The light bulb to the dim bulb.

But this was, after all, the eighties.

The former anchorman walked along the beach at Wellfleet on Cape Cod as he narrated Clifford's adventure:

> Divers have been bringing up treasure for a couple of years, but it is the promise of what might yet be uncovered that could make this salvage operation important to both archaeologists and historians. For the first time it may help us see how the pirates lived. Were they really the villains of the story books—rapacious brigands or swash-buckling buccaneers?
>
> She was named the *Whydah* [Widda], a British slave ship, heavily armed and carrying tons of gold, silver, indigo and ivory. She was coming up from the Caribbean where she had probably traded a load of slaves for precious cargo. She was spotted by a British pirate, "Black" Sam Bellamy. He gave chase, and three days later, she gave up without a fight. Black Bellamy liked her better than his own ship so he transferred to her the cargo from some fifty merchant vessels he had previously plundered, put some extra cannons aboard, and headed toward Cape Cod, where legend has it he had a young lover. But on the night of April 26th, 1717, in a blistering storm, the *Whydah* broke up on a sandbar along the Massachusetts coast. It was a graveyard of many ships over the years. Black Sam probably died in that storm, but a few pirates lived to tell the tale.
>
> It's a tale that has taken on special meaning to Barry Clifford, entrepreneur and salvage expert, the president of Maritime Explorations Incorporated. He found the wreck that others had sought for more than

two and a half centuries, and he did it through some intensive work in libraries and state archives.

Maybe it was Cronkite's voice in the background, but on the screen Barry Clifford appeared more substantial. Wearing a leather bomber jacket and a blue baseball cap, he looked and talked like a real adventurer. Clifford described to Cronkite what that intensive research had revealed.

In May 1717, when news of the wreck reached Boston, the colonial governor sent his own salvor, Captain Cyprian Southack, to recover the pirates' booty. Although Captain Southack was unsuccessful, he drew a map to the wreck and provided additional clues in letters to the governor: the *Whydah* was twenty-five miles from Provincetown, three miles from Billingsgate [Wellfleet], and two miles from Samuel Harding's house. As Clifford recited the clues, video graphics triangulated the position on a modern map of Cape Cod. "And this is the area where we staked our claim."

As Southack wrote, and Clifford proved: "*The Riches with the Guns will be buried in the sand.*"

Cronkite's special continued, but I was no longer paying attention. I watched the packager, who was back behind his desk shuffling papers. I was still baffled by Clifford and Cronkite together, but mostly I wondered how a story worthy of a CBS News special could have ended up here among the cookbooks. I flattered myself that it was waiting for me.

Seeing that nobody was watching the tape, Lief got up and flicked off the VCR. Barry Clifford sat up straight and rolled his shoulders, stretching his neck. I had given back *The New York Times*, and he gestured with it as he spoke. Something was different about him. Something obscured by the waving newspaper. I couldn't figure out what it was, but I was sitting forward, suddenly tense.

12

"I am a free Prince," Clifford said. "And I have as much right to make war on the whole world as he who has a hundred ships at sea, and an army of 100,000 in the field: and this my conscience tells me. But there is no arguing with such sniveling puppies, who allow their superiors to kick them about deck with pleasure; and pin their faith upon a pimp of a parson; a squab who neither practices nor believes what he puts upon the chuckle-headed fools he preaches to."

The packager stared at me. Clifford stared upward, his eyes far away. *The blob of spit was gone!* There was more to this treasure hunter than I thought.

Clifford plopped the newspaper on the coffee table.

"That was Black Sam Bellamy's most famous speech—the pirate's creed." Clifford paused. He watched me intently. "Bellamy's crew declared they were Robin Hood's men," he said slowly, then sped up. "Most people don't realize that pirates sailed under written constitutions called Articles. Signing the Article gave pirates freedom and equality. English, French, Dutch, African, Native American: it made no difference. There were fifty Blacks aboard the *Whydah* and a handful of Indians. They each got a vote. The treasure was divided equally."

Clifford grinned. "Well, not exactly," he said. "The Captain got two shares."

I grinned back, and Clifford got rolling again: "Arguments were settled with pistols, and anyone who cheated was marooned. They had life insurance for widows and workmen's comp for the wounded. Of course if you got caught, you got hanged; so the Articles were signed in blood."

Now Clifford was staring right at me, no longer smiling. "The South Sea Company, which was the equivalent of Ford Motors, was in the slave business: stealing people and calling them cargo. With our present understanding of freedom, every red-blooded American would be flying a skull and crossbones."

Clifford's tale went on. The pirate Sam Bellamy fell in love with a 15-year-old Cape Cod beauty, Maria Hallett, and needed money to marry, when word reached Cape Cod that a fleet of Spanish treasure galleons had wrecked off Florida. Bellamy and his partner, Paulgrave Williams, then sailed for the wrecks in a leaky old sloop. When they failed to find treasure, they went "on the account" as pirates. During their short careers, they were two of the most successful pirates in history.

Clifford told about a trial in Boston, about exhortations to the condemned pirates by the Reverend Cotton Mather, about the hanging of six pirates at Charlestown Ferry, and about how Maria Hallett went mad. She became the witch of Wellfleet, ensnaring sailors with potion-laced doughnuts and then riding them across the waves like dolphins.

And, of course, she put a curse on the wreck.

About his search for Bellamy's flagship, Clifford said he began dreaming about the wreck as a child, hearing pirate stories from his Uncle Bill, a fisherman on the Cape. When Clifford was 37 years old, in 1982, he set out to find it. The first traces of the wreck—some clay pipe stems and a chisel-point nail—he discovered while diving with John F. Kennedy, Jr.

Clifford said that he used the nail and pipe stems to get a permit for the site while he assembled a gang of his own. He went to Aspen, Colorado, where his best friend and college roommate, Rob McClung, was chief of police. Through McClung, Clifford met a local judge, John Levin, who rode with McClung on drug raids. The judge introduced Clifford to the largest landowner in Vail, and soon Maritime Explorations, Inc., was launched. Their corporation was modeled after the pirate Articles.

In the summer of 1983, Clifford left his wife and children on Martha's Vineyard and moved with his gang into an old sea captain's house on Cape Cod. As their boat was refitted for salvage, they trained together—running, swimming, pumping weights, and pounding heavy bags—to prepare for the diving. *People* magazine showed up, and the divers were never lonely. Soon Clifford met his own "Maria Hallett," a 19-year-old magazine cover girl named Heidi who grew up on the Cape. "On our first date we listened to folk tales from a barefoot old schoolteacher and searched graveyards for more clues."

Clifford leaned back in his chair with a self-satisfied smile. I rubbed my neck, collecting myself. I had completely misjudged this guy. My instincts were not usually so wrong, and I was playing catchup.

"The book will need details." I said. "These are fine anecdotes, but the reader will need to know what it felt like— what the light was like. What's the most vivid scene you can remember?"

Clifford thought about it.

"It was after midnight at a dive bar called the Beachcomber. We decided to test the security of our salvage ship *Vast Explorer II*. We painted our faces black and rowed out through the breakers in a rubber dingy. There was no moon. It was pitch black. We scaled the side of the *Vast* with our teeth clenched on rubber daggers. John-John Kennedy was dancing alone to Santana under the spotlight on the stern deck."

Clifford let the image hang in the air between us.

"But we couldn't see the second crewman, a Special Forces veteran armed with an assault rifle. We had to hope he would get the joke."

"And if he hadn't?" I asked.

The treasure hunter yawned. He was playing me like a tuna. He grimaced and got out of his chair, stretching his neck again.

"Diving accident?" I asked.

"Yeah, sort of."

"Me too." I rubbed my neck. "Skydiving. Bad case of whiplash."

The packager picked it up. "That was a piece for *Sports Illustrated*."

So the packager did read. I had underestimated both of these men.

Now Lief wanted me to tell Clifford the skydiving story. As I did, Clifford paced, stretching his neck.

It was about the bandit parachute jump into Shea Stadium during the infamous sixth game of the '86 World Series. The stunt, while spectacular, was not risky. The jumper flying the *Go Mets* banner was an actor, and he got famous. The man who intrigued me, however, was the unknown pilot—who risked his license and possibly his livelihood for a stunt he could never talk about. Why? The question really bugged me. The FAA subpoenaed a lot of people and jailed the jumper for contempt, but no one would talk. So I took a jump, danced with a guy, took a punch—and ended up meeting a much more interesting hero who hadn't been written up in *The New York Times*. The parachute story was an almost polite way of telling Clifford he was full of shit.

Clifford sat down and picked up his water glass. He watched me over the rim.

"That's a good story," he said.

"It's time for lunch," said Phillip Lief.

The Pirate Prince

People have diddled at the *Whidah* for literally centuries, rejuvenating the mystery of her lost treasure, embellishing and illuminating its transition from history to legend. Even Thoreau is said to have written of coins from the wreck found washed up on the beach. That's more than one hundred years after, but Thoreau was a romantic, just the right sort to turn mere events into thrills of perception. Thoreau had himself found a coin, but it was of Louis XIV, dated 1741, which indicates 24 post mortem years of literary license.

—the log of archaeologist Edwin
Dethlefsen, Ph.D., 1983

Back in college it was a point of pride that I wouldn't do anything drunk that I wouldn't do sober. I wouldn't take advantage of myself like that, or anybody else. Late one night during my sophomore year, a woman I had pursued shamelessly and with an embarrassing lack of progress tiptoed into my room, crawled into my lower bunk, and passed out beside me. There she was. She was dressed from the dance in the dining hall. She smelled of perfume and sweat and drink. She was lovely. My hand moved above her as if stroking her aura, but I couldn't touch her. Finally she lurched upright, stared at me in astonishment, and bolted out of the room.

As Clifford, Lief, and I sat down at a nearby pasta restaurant, a plan began to take shape in my head. I ordered a gin and tonic and downed it. Maybe I *could* do this book. I ordered a glass of wine. Something was wrong with Clifford's story or it never would have washed up among the cookbooks. Writing the book *with* Clifford was destined for disaster— like the time I tried to kayak through the culvert hoping to break through the wire fence at the downstream end. Nevertheless, my plan was worth checking out. After more wine, it would seem a stroke of genius. Meanwhile, Clifford drank a light beer and then switched to soda.

His story continued.

That first summer of diving, in 1983, was a time of disappointment, conflict, and hardship. Other than the chisel-point nail and the pipe stems, the only artifacts found were a rudder strap and a mizzen stay. Meanwhile, rival treasure hunters—"claim jumpers"—filed their own permits on either side of Clifford's area. By September his first archaeologist quit, and by November, as the weather closed in, his crew despaired. Rob McClung came home one day to find Clifford, stark naked, chasing Heidi with a duck call. That was too much even for Aspen's former police chief, and so he quit and took Judge Levin with him. McClung and Levin were then set up with a house and a Ferrari in Malibu to write a TV series about their drug raids in Aspen. They returned to the treasure hunt only because their patron was cut in half with two clips from a machine gun.

I sat back and grinned. This book might be fun.

"It was crazy, silly, and stupid." Clifford said, grinning back. "My parents wouldn't have anything to do with me. We were writing bad checks for fuel." Clifford chuckled. "That first Halloween the Captain of the *Vast Explorer* was so broke that he drew a picture of a pumpkin for his kids.

"We never thought there would be a tomorrow. We figured we'd all end up broke or in jail. We kept going because the press built it up so much. Not to find it would have been devastating. We dug and dove. Just went for it."

On July 19, 1984, Rob McClung dove into a new pit and saw the tops of two cannons protruding from the sand. Beside them was a cannon ball, which the former police chief brought to the surface. "Ghostbusters" played on the radio. Clifford then scraped the encrustation from the ball and found a silver coin. Lightning flashed. In one pit were hundreds of coins as well as gold dust, like chocolate in fudge ripple ice cream. Treasure, stored in battery boxes, was soon spilling out from under Clifford's bed.

The adventure was just beginning.

In Provincetown, where the first cannon was to be brought ashore, one of the "claim jumpers" was waiting. A Portuguese fisherman, Matt Costa had one eye blown out by a shotgun. A pirate-like figure, he wore a black patch. As the cannon was lowered on ropes into a pickup truck, Costa revealed a pistol and ordered the crane operator to stop. Undaunted, Clifford leaped into the truck like Errol Flynn and severed the ropes with his knife. The cannon dropped into the bed, and they drove off with Costa in hot pursuit.

Clifford grinned at me, and I grinned back. Old pirates, new pirates, Kennedys, cover girls, witches, machine guns, cannons, treasure, and now a car chase.

Clifford took special pleasure in an anecdote about the discovery of the ship's bell. Before then, the name of the pirate ship had been spelled *Whidah*. Knocking off the encrustation on the bell, however, exposed an inscription: *The Whydah Gally 1716*.

"Change the prospectus!" Clifford had said.

"Prospectus, Hell!" roared an associate. "I'll have to change my tattoo!"

The bell was the absolute proof Clifford needed for a major stock offering to finance a full-scale archaeological excavation of the wreck site. "Wall Streeters," Clifford said, "had tremendous defense mechanisms to prevent them from investing in something as ridiculous as a pirate treasure," he explained. "But underneath, they were all kids following the psychology of the neighborhood. 'Here are my marbles, here are yours,' I told them. 'Want to play?' Put that way, the Wall Streeters were soon saying 'Don't leave me out.'"

In 1987, E.F. Hutton raised $6 million dollars for the project, the first time a major Wall Street firm had financed a treasure hunt. That deal was orchestrated by the partners of a company called Silver Screen Partners, which had financed the last four years of Walt Disney movies.

In his vault at the Bank of New England, Clifford already had $40 million dollars worth of treasure. At his conservation lab, he had more than one hundred thousand artifacts. His archaeologists were reconstructing a pirate: from boot to sock to tibia to belt buckle to buttons to scarf to pistol. The bits and pieces had been "concreted" to the cannon that may have crushed the pirate during the wreck.

And the mother lode was still to come.

Clifford's only remaining obstacle was the archaeological community, and he got heated as he talked about it. "I hired archaeologists only because Massachusetts forced me to, but I got the best. My first, a Harvard Ph.D. named Ted Dethlefsen, was president of the Society for Historical Archaeology. Even after we had won all our legal battles with the state, we continued to do careful archaeology on the site."

"How come?"

"The future is archaeology for profit," Clifford said, rolling his shoulders. "I have built the largest lab in the business, which will become a center for archaeology. It's a competitive thing, and I'll use every trick in the business." His blue eyes were steady. "I'm more dangerous than any tiger shark."

Our lunch was ending, and Phillip Lief was smiling. So was Clifford. So was I. Lief paid the check, Clifford smoothed the pages of his newspaper, and I closed my notebook. I felt lightheaded from both the booze and the story and left the restaurant fighting down the temptation to offer to write the book on the spot. Instead, I asked the packager who would write the proposal.

"Nobody." Lief was still smiling.

"Huh?"

Lief explained that he had arranged for Clifford to meet with seven different publishers over the next two days. Clifford would repeat his story for all seven, and then the publishers would have a week to submit bids. Jacqueline Kennedy Onassis, a senior editor at Doubleday, was throwing a cocktail party at her apartment the following evening. Since John-John had been one of Clifford's divers, Doubleday was the best bet. Second best was Random House. Robert Bernstein, chairman of the board, helped with publicity for the wreck, and his son Tom was a partner at Silver Screen Partners.

We had connections, to say the least.

"But won't the publishers need to see something on paper?" I asked, completely missing the point. What made me think that anything I could put on paper would be more persuasive than Barry Clifford, in person, brandishing a fresh copy of *The New York Times*?

As we walked back toward Lief's office, I realized that I wouldn't be invited to the cocktail party at Jackie O's. I had to remind myself that I hadn't agreed to write the book.

Clifford and I parted with Lief at the entrance to his building. As the two of us continued west, Clifford told me about his days in college when he threw the javelin. All he had wanted in the world then was to make the Olympic team.

At the corner of 20th Street and Fifth Avenue, Clifford wrote down my phone number and said he'd call as soon as the meetings with the publishers were over. We shook hands. For a moment our eyes met—which I found surprisingly destabilizing. Then we pulled back and there was a moment of what seemed mutual appraisal. For me, it was like being at a regatta, sizing up the competition on the dock before climbing into the shells. Could I take him? I wondered. I was fifteen years younger, seven inches taller, and thirty pounds heavier. But Clifford was a plug of muscle—more dangerous than a tiger shark.

He could inflict serious damage. I sensed that. But he would be unfamiliar with rowers—men used to toiling backwards, blindly, trained, most of all, to endure.

A Plan Emerges

Such a day rum all out; our company somewhat
sober; a damned confusion among us; rogues a-
plotting; great talk of separation; so I looked sharply
for a prize.

—the log of Edward Teach, a.k.a.
Blackbeard, 1718

It was only hour or so later that I was uptown on West
85th Street, standing in front of a refurbished tenement, late
as usual. I glanced toward Central Park, took a couple steps
in that direction, and then backtracked. When you've walked
off a cliff there are two schools of thought: you can flap your
arms or you can scream. Whichever you choose makes no
difference on the outcome but says something about you. The
philosophy professor who imparted that bit of wisdom to me
also said that there are certain questions you simply don't

ask. You don't wake up every morning and ask yourself if you love your wife, because sooner or later the answer is going to be no. Your prior commitment to the marriage makes the question irrelevant and vaguely dishonorable.

I stepped down the small flight of brick steps, turned to face the security camera, and rang the bell.

Nothing happened. A few moments later a carpenter opened the door going out. The workman was wondering whether he should let me into the building when I went past him. I could feel his eyes on my back as I trudged down the hall, punched the numbers into the lock on the door at the end, and let myself into the waiting room. The three chairs were empty. *Shit.*

I pushed through the next door into a ten-foot-square office. The far wall had windows looking out on a concrete patio enclosed by chain link topped with razor wire. The left wall of the office had a daybed. The other two walls were lined with bookshelves. My wife and the therapist sat facing each other on identical chrome and leather recliners. They rotated to face me.

I met my wife five years before at *American Health* magazine. It was February 1984 and freezing. Jennifer had just returned to Manhattan, almost broke after two wild years of modeling with Elite in Paris, and she arrived at my dreary, seven-by-seven-foot cubicle like sunrise on the ocean: six feet of blonde, blue-eyed, radiant energy. Two days late for our cover "go-see," but what the hell. I looked at the covers in her portfolio. Her face lit *Vogue Italia.* In a bathing suit her body splashed *Life.* In white lace she graced *Brides.* She had put on fifteen pounds since her last fashion cover, and so she looked in real life the way models do in pictures. Her image would create the best-sellers of *American Health.*

At that time I was four months away from the '84 Olympic trials, doing everything I could think of to justify my salary while I trained. Sacrifice was not high on my list of priorities, and so I had arranged a special training junket—to compete with an *American Health* triathlon relay team in the first Bahamas Diamond Triathlon of the Stars, on Paradise Island. The magazine was sending three athletes and a photographer, all expenses paid.

And so it happened that just before Jennifer walked into my office, the swimmer from my relay team called to cancel because of an injury. I needed a replacement, fast. Meanwhile, Jennifer scanned my story board.

"What's this triathlon?" she asked.

A setup like that comes only once every few lifetimes. I wasn't about to screw it up.

"Can you swim?" I asked.

"Sure. I was on a team as a kid."

"Would you like to go to the Bahamas?"

The day before the triathlon, I needed to scout the bike course around the island, and Jennifer wanted to come along. Sure, I said. But there wasn't room in the budget for two motor-scooters, so she'd have to hold on to me. That night on the beach, I almost forgot that I was nearly engaged to a woman who had just left for a new job in Paris. The next day Jennifer swam a mile and a half in big surf, emerged like a mermaid, and I forgot completely. With Jennifer smiling on the dock, it hardly mattered when I lost the Olympic trials. A month later, we were engaged. She was not only a model, but a talented photographer. I bought her a new Nikon, and so when Avon wasn't paying her $2,500 a day, other models and actors came to our apartment for head shots. She could shoot two or three in an afternoon and charge $400 for each.

But right now her eyes were like ice.

I took a seat on the daybed. "Where are we?"

"*We* were talking about your buying that house on the lake," said the therapist. A balding, bearded gnome in his late forties, Peter could afford to smile solicitously. He had me by the balls.

The path that brought us to Peter began when Jennifer decided to make the leap from print modeling to acting. She went to a series of coaches. She could walk and talk, and the camera loved her, but she could not cry. She was "blocked." And so one of her coaches suggested a therapist named Linda. My wife was reluctant, but she went. She took to it.

She soon dropped the acting classes, preferring to make quick money doing commercials, but she continued with Linda. Soon she and Linda seemed tighter than we were. In due course my wife decided that we needed a therapist. She got Peter's name from Linda.

I had been to a psychiatrist for depression shortly after coming to New York. I went twice a week for four months and learned that my parents' divorce had been my parents' problem. That I had little memory for pain was a coping mechanism—and apparently an empowering one. Not to worry. Once the psychiatrist and I started talking mostly about real estate, we agreed it was time to quit.

With Peter we started out talking real estate, which was just fine. As I recall, his previous office had been a group practice in a rental building on Central Park West. When that building was sold to its tenants as a co-op, he managed to rid himself of his partners and then sued the building to use his professional lease to buy the office at the insider price. That office was now his residence. Currently, he was renovating his home, as well as this new office complex on West 85th. He had put money down on a yet-to-be-built condo in Key

West.

I thought I knew where Peter was coming from and could deal with it for a few months. By the mid eighties the only thing that stood between a true Manhattanite and jail was his accountant. It seemed only appropriate that a marriage therapist would try immediately to get to the real heart of things. Get to where you lived, so to speak. Intimate sexual details could be pried out of most anyone over the course of a subway ride.

But then, several weeks into therapy, Peter mentioned on our way out the door that he was getting married that weekend.

"Congratulations," I said. "Who's the lucky bride?"

Linda.

I was screwed. Now, more than a year later, we were going twice a week: Eight hundred bucks a month to Peter on top of the seven hundred my wife paid Linda in the adjacent office. Peter estimated that we had a fifty-fifty chance of saving our marriage and suggested extra individual sessions with me.

Peter leaned back in his recliner and clasped his hands behind his head. He came from a long line of lawyers. "You two are already burning the candle at both ends," he said. "You don't need another mortgage."

He was right about that, but it wasn't that simple.

And I had a plan.

"The lake house is only $175,000," I answered. "My consulting contract with Nike still pays three grand a month; *American Health* still sells my videos; and the final payment on my how-to book will bring in $7,500 as soon as I finish it. Besides, I just got offered the down payment."

I had their attention.

I told them about Cronkite, the Kennedys, E. F. Hutton, and the Hollywood connection through Silver Screen Partners. "I'll get twenty-five grand just for signing the contract. Another twenty when I'm done. Plus a share of the movie rights. The treasure hunter kept a log during the adventure, so writing the book will be a snap. After this, I'll be able to get an advance on a book of my own." I looked at my wife and smiled. "We could buy a ski boat."

That last card was a trump. A rower, I hated ski boats, but my wife had wanted one ever since her dad hadn't let her drive his. If the therapist got between my wife and her boat, he would be history. If we bought the lake house and the ski boat, we wouldn't be able to afford therapy. We would stop scraping away at our marriage before it was too late. All I had to do was sign on with Clifford.

It was a crazy and stupid plan, but as we said at Nike, *Just do it!*

By the time the session dragged to an end, the therapist thought the lake house wasn't such a bad idea after all, and my wife and I left holding hands. We caught a cab home.

West 79th Street was solidly fashionable and extremely convenient. With four lanes plus room on either side for parking, the street spread as wide and airy as the avenues and without the traffic. At the east end of our block, at Columbus Avenue, multimillion-dollar apartments in Zeckendorf's new tower rose above shops like Laura Ashley. Across Columbus, 79th Street ended at the Museum of Natural History, just before Central Park. My racing bicycle had been stolen, and so I now rode the six-mile Central Park loop on my mountain bike, a knobby-tired clunker that squeaked and rattled as if a mockingbird had nested in the chain. I had planned to buy a new racing bike, but it turned out to be so much fun squeaking and rattling past the other racers on the loop that I never did. At the west end of our block, at Amsterdam Avenue, the corner deli supplied my coffee and bagel each morning. Further west was Broadway (only a block from Zabar's), West End Avenue, Riverside Drive, Riverside Park, and the Boat Basin on the Hudson River. Before I saw the lake house, a long-range plan had been to buy a houseboat in the Basin. Most of them rested on the river bottom, rotting in sludge from their own heads, but it would be worth buying one to get the boat slip and the free parking place that went with it. I could then sell the houseboat or sink it and have a place to store a rowing shell.

Our building, the Manchester House, had a stone and wrought-iron facade that looked vaguely Gothic, like the buildings at Yale. After a couple of stories, the stone gave way to brick and climbed for fifteen more. A sprinkling of stone window treatments up the face made the building appear both handsome and unassuming. Right now, however, the steel bars and wood planks of a scaffolding blocked the facade. Underneath the scaffolding the sidewalk felt like a cave.

We entered to the sound of cursing: a shoving match at our front door.

"Just let me get my goddamned tools!"

I recognized the *faux bois* painter who had been working on the lobby. With one shoulder jammed against the outside of the iron gate, he was putting his legs to work. Inside the vestibule, wedged between the wall and the gate, was our doorman, who couldn't quite get the thing latched. He had threatened to call the police but couldn't move to the phone. His new uniform was wrinkled. One epaulette hung askew.

I tapped the painter sharply on the shoulder, and he spun

around to swing. He stopped. A member of the co-op's board of directors, I owned more shares than anyone else in the building. If he hit me, he would never get paid. He would probably never get paid anyway.

"I'll get your tools," I said.

He stood away.

The doorman straightened his uniform, touched his cap and opened the gate.

The rich mahogany-colored *faux bois* of the lobby was on the neighborhood tour when it was new, in 1927. But a series of landlords had let the wood-grain paint deteriorate until the entrance was like a railroad tunnel. In the late seventies, the final landlord cashed out—selling the apartments to the tenants for $10,000 to $35,000. In the early eighties, the building began to be refurbished: new wiring, new plumbing, and a new roof. Money for such work poured in because the prices of the apartments went up tenfold, and every time an apartment changed hands, the building took five percent of the profit. Repainting the lobby was to be the crown jewel of the restoration.

But the same night the co-op board announced the $80,000 lobby renovation, our engineer informed us that the steel understructure of the building was rusting through. The scaffolding went up to catch bricks that might drop from the facade while we figured out what to do. Meanwhile, the real estate market collapsed around us, and the contractor who hired the *faux bois* painter skipped town. We had to keep the painter out of the lobby because he might try to destroy his work just to get even.

My wife took the elevator to prepare to take some actor's head shot, while I fetched the painter's tools and walked him to the corner. He left cursing, but he left.

When we moved into the building, in 1984, the elevator

ended in a purple hallway between the two small penthouses, but we bought both and gutted them. We met our neighbors for three floors down when a jackhammer went through a water pipe while making room for the Jacuzzi. But after two years the major work was done. The elevator had a key lock opposite the PH button. You turned the key and pressed the button. Half a minute later the door slid open into a two-bedroom Adirondack cabin in the sky. Everything was natural and handmade: clear pine paneled the walls, white oak covered the floors, mahogany framed the windows and French doors, smooth creek stones lined the fireplace, slender tree trunks supported the log mantle, and granite topped the kitchen counters. Even the refrigerator, a Sub Zero, was paneled in clear pine. On the wraparound terrace, giant redwood planters supported birch trees and a crop of wild strawberries.

My architect, who had taken the upper bunk at Yale, had designed the Brinkley/Joel residence. His favorite place was a camp in the Adirondaks, and he'd put his heart into the design of this apartment.

So had I.

That day, when the elevator opened into the foyer, I was blasted by hot air. In the living room, all three pairs of French doors had been flung open to get the most sunlight for the photo shoot. From the terrace my wife cursed the shadows. When we bought the penthouse, a gap in the wall of buildings across the street gave us an unobstructed view downtown—and perfect southern light for shooting. Then a condo went up in the gap. And up. And up. Still virtually empty, the condo teetered on the brink of bankruptcy. Now the only major building we could see downtown was Citicorp, a spire like a middle finger that held our mortgage.

I made a hard right away from the living room.

The varnished pine door before me was flanked by an original woodcut of an eight-oared crew, the illustration from my review in *The New York Times Book Review*. Below it was my photo, in rowing shorts, from *Andy Warhol's Interview*. Above the door was a drawing from the Oxford-Cambridge Boat Race, the artwork from my piece in *The New Yorker*.

I banged opened the door.

The room beyond, my office, had rotten plaster walls, peeling paint, steel-barred windows, and a ceiling threatening to cave in. The before picture. I had bugged my old roommate about finishing the design — maybe with an Adirondack lean-to on the back terrace. But he had pushed me instead toward Maya Lin, our friend from Yale who designed the Viet Nam Memorial in Washington, D.C. It made no sense. Now a freelancer, Tim needed the work. He just couldn't get it done. Finally, after the annual black-tie rowing dinner at the Metropolitan Club, he said he needed to talk. Of Irish descent, Tim stood six-feet, nine-inches and told the very tallest of tales. Looking at him was like looking into a mirror. Everyone thought we were brothers. Freshman year, I had beaten him for a seat in the first boat, and he had quit the crew to concentrate on art. He sang opera and danced in Balanchine's master classes. But that night as we sat at the bar he talked about nothing for much too long. Then he said simply. "I'm HIV-positive. I have been for quite some time. Too long."

I stood in the center of my office shedding clothes. A pair of rowing shorts lay wadded on the floor, and I scooped them up and slipped them on. The portable CD player held the Talking Heads' *Stop Making Sense*. I clicked over "Psycho Killer," "Swamp," and "Slippery People" to "Burning Down the House," climbed on my rowing ergometer, and started to pull — losing myself in the rhythm of sweat and pain.

Layers of Proof

Every journalist who is not too stupid or too full of himself to notice what is going on knows that what he does is morally indefensible. He is a kind of confidence man, preying on people's vanity, ignorance and loneliness, gaining their trust and betraying them without remorse. Like the credulous widow who wakes up one day to find the charming young man and all her savings gone, so the consenting subject of a piece of nonfiction writing learns—when the article or book appears—*his* hard lesson.

—Janet Malcolm, *The New Yorker,*
March 13, 1989

Twenty minutes later, purged and sopped with sweat, I emerged from my office long enough to grab a Corona from the Sub Zero. Coming back in, I found the mess startling. Sweat puddled under the rowing ergometer. Stacks of paper, boxes of videotapes and damp clothes covered the floor. My desk, an oak monster painted with green latex, lay buried under beer bottles and coffee mugs. I plopped myself down on the almost matching green chair and felt around under the papers for my Swiss Army knife. When I found it, I popped the cap on the Corona, and snapped it spinning like a flying saucer toward the Slovenian flag hanging on the far wall. What a dump!

Other than the Macintosh computer and laser printer, almost everything in the room had been salvaged, finagled, or pilfered. The desk, chair, and mismatched metal filing cabinets were intercepted on voyages to the landfill. The bookshelf and ceiling fan had been abandoned by the apartment's previous owner. The fax machine came free from Nike, and with luck they had forgotten it. The rowing ergometer came free from Concept II in Vermont, because I photographed it for a how-to book. The Slovenian flag was liberated from a light pole at the '79 World Rowing Championship in Bled, Yugoslavia. An older teammate snagged the big flag with five circles from Montreal in '76. The night after the finals he lured an East German girl under the flag pole and made a such a spectacle of his passion that the guard turned away long enough for him to lower the flag and stuff it under her blouse. I hadn't planned to steal the big flag in Moscow. I planned to pin it—just like the grand old city flag of Nottingham, England. After winning that regatta, my Yale crew climbed the wall of the castle, disabled the security loop on the flagpole, dropped the flag, and pinned a Y with crossed oars to it. We raised the flag again. Perfect victory.

I finished my beer, added the bottle to the collection on the desk and began to search the stacks of papers for a manila envelope filled with press clippings about Barry Clifford. The packager sent the clippings prior to the meeting, but I had only skimmed them. I hadn't really wanted to read the story beforehand and had misplaced the clippings before I could. Some people work in a disaster area and know where everything is. Not me. My life is squarely on the side of entropy, and entropy is still winning.

Eureka! I pulled out the clippings from a file labeled Take Out menus and thumbed through them.

On top was a front-page story from *The New York Times*, headlined "Bell Provides Identification of Pirate Ship for First Time." According to the *Times*, "Mr. Clifford appears to have established irrefutably the provenance of thousands of coins and hundreds of pounds of other artifacts as well as the fate of the *Whydah*..." The *Times* suggested that the value of the treasure could run into the hundreds of millions of dollars.

Next was a cover story from *Parade* magazine with a picture of Clifford, headlined: "The Man Who Discovered a $400 Million Pirate Treasure." After that was a cover of *People*. The small photo of Clifford and the President's son had the headline: "John Kennedy & Co. Dive for Pirate Gold." Also among the clippings was a letter from Senator Edward Kennedy to the President of the Azores, praising Clifford's company for its record of careful archaeology. The most recent clipping was from the front page of the *Boston Globe*: "Staking a Claim to Tea Party: Explorer says he has located ornate chests."

Clifford was a story. But what kind?

I picked up the phone and called Chip McGrath, my editor at *The New Yorker*. McGrath edited the Talk of the Town section. He knew something about almost everything and was interested in the rest. McGrath was also one of those rare editors who have the courtesy and backbone to say no quickly. He returned the call almost immediately.

"What's up?" McGrath's voice had the enthusiasm of a

fossil—probably the result of having to say no all the time. But he was a hockey player (Yale '68) and had Rollerbladed through the halls of *The New Yorker*. He wasn't half as dead as he pretended to be.

"I got an idea."

"Shoot."

I started to tell him about Clifford, but he already knew. No surprise there. What stunned me is that McGrath thought a profile of Clifford was my best idea yet. Two staff writers had prior claims to the piece, but if they passed, I would have a good chance of an assignment.

If I could have dropped the book project right then, I probably would have. But it was too late. Now that the book was being peddled to publishers, Clifford wouldn't tell his story to a *New Yorker* writer.

"I'm thinking about writing a book with Clifford," I told McGrath.

I think I stunned him. "You can't do that," he said.

"Why not?"

"You're a journalist. Besides, authorized biographies always go wrong."

I then called Roger Kennedy, class of '49 and director of the National Museum of American History at the Smithsonian Institution in Washington, D.C. I had met Roger when he hosted the gala boycott party for the '80 Olympic team at his museum. After the party I quit rowing cold turkey and moved to a thatched-roof cottage on the coast of Ireland, hoping to write a novel. Instead, I munched hallucinogenic mushrooms, read Dostoyevski, and wrote a suicidal short story, which I sent to Kennedy. For me, and I suppose in general, making the Olympic team was about tapping forces and instincts it would be nobler to ignore. You climb a mountain, shedding everything and everyone as you go; and then you make it to the top and realize you're alone, isolated and basically a jerk. But Roger wrote back. It was a long letter. A magical statement saying yes, there are connections between people as real and as powerful and as good as oars locked into water. Shortly afterward I got a telegram from my agent saying that my senior-year Scholar of the House project, *The Shell Game,* had been bought by a publisher. When the book came out, Kennedy wrote the president of NBC, a letter that turned into an interview with Jane Pauley on the *Today Show.* Kennedy also called one of his classmates, who had made *Psychology Today* such a huge success in the late sixties and seventies. Soon after that call I had a job as an editor at the start-up *American Health.*

Kennedy lived in a bigger world, and he looked after me.

Now I wanted to know what Kennedy thought about a *Whydah* book—and whether he would consider a special Smithsonian exhibition on pirates. I figured that artifacts from the only pirate ship ever excavated could be the basis for a major show, which in turn could sell thousands of books. I was not expecting much enthusiasm. To me pirates seemed like kid stuff—but not to Roger Kennedy.

While he had never heard of Clifford or the *Whydah,* Kennedy had several volumes on pirates in his personal library. Pirates were "proto-revolutionaries," he said. The democratic traditions of the pirates during America's colonial period may have been significant to the creation of the United States. He thought the exhibit was promising and referred me to his maritime curator, Paul Johnston.

My call to Johnston snaked its way through every switch in the Smithsonian, tracing the history of wired communication until I was sure that the maritime curator was talking through a tin can tied to a string. I could barely hear him at first and was sorry when I did.

"I was just talking to Roger Kennedy about an exhibit of artifacts from the *Whydah*. Would that be difficult?"

"Not difficult," Johnston said. "Impossible."

"You're joking?"

"Not at all. The artifacts were found by treasure hunters. Most major museums, including the Smithsonian, have signed an agreement not to display any artifacts found by treasure hunters. Pretty soon auction houses won't even sell them."

"But the *Whydah* is the only pirate ship ever found. Why not let people see it?"

"That's not the point. We had a professor from Illinois give a talk here about the gold jewelry from the *Whydah*. Had I known about it earlier, I would have canceled it."

My older brother, Brady, had trained as a classical archaeologist at Swarthmore and Cal Berkeley. He learned ancient Greek and Latin—not to mention modern Greek, French, German, Turkish, and four or five others—but his biggest smile came after digging up a life-size marble sculpture in Turkey. He finally gave up archaeology because he wanted to make a living and because he couldn't stand the politics and bureaucratic nightmares. He joined the State Department. I was beginning to understand why.

"I like Clifford personally," Johnston continued in a way that made me sure he hated Clifford's guts. "But what he is doing is wrong. His company relies on ridiculous hyperbole and defends itself with a battery of lawyers. When I worked at Harvard's Peabody Museum, I stood up against Clifford at a public meeting, and my boss got a threatening note from Clifford's lawyer."

"Clifford found the *Whydah*, didn't he?"

"Yeah, eventually," Johnston conceded. "What matters is

the way he operates. Check out his grand plan to dive for the chests from the Boston Tea Party. There was a big announcement on the front page of the *Boston Globe.*"

"Why?"

"Because the Tea Party site is under landfill, beneath a Boston Edison substation."

Before we hung up, Johnston gave me the phone number of an archaeologist in New Hampshire named Warren Riess, who had once worked on the *Whydah*. When I called him and mentioned Clifford, Riess almost hung up. I dropped *The New Yorker,* and he changed his mind.

"My colleagues warned me not to work with Clifford," Reiss said. "And they were right. Being an archaeologist on a treasure hunt is like being an environmentalist on a whaling ship. Treasure hunters get boats, women, houses, and cars by using shipwrecks as con games."

"Is the *Whydah* a con?"

Riess hesitated. "No," he said. "The project's real."

"How do you know?"

"Vertical stratigraphy. The artifacts were distributed on different layers of sand. Had the artifacts been salted (hidden by the treasure hunter to hoodwink investors) they would have been on the same layer?"

"Couldn't they have been salted in different layers?"

"Not a chance. I dove on the site and saw artifacts spilling from the sides of the pit. They found the *Whydah.* It's a shame, but they did."

My last call was to my agent. I told him yes: I would do the pirate book with Clifford—But on one condition: the book packager must agree to let me work on a *New Yorker* profile of Clifford at the same time. My agent said he would work it out, and so I headed for the shower.

WALKING THE PLANK

The next evening Clifford phoned me from the cocktail party at Jackie O's. All of the meetings had gone well, he said. All seven publishers would bid for the book. I asked him about the magazine profile, and he was thrilled. This was a better plan than I ever could have hoped for. I then called the realtor in the Catskills to put in an offer on the lake house and phoned the garage to have them bring down the Jeep for the weekend. Too bad the Mercedes was broken. It would be great to take the top down.

Stalks and Bonds

Up with the Jolly Roger Barry Clifford is a professional treasure hunter, one of those guys in the wet suits you see on *National Geographic* programs coming up with fistfuls of doubloons draped in seaweed. Among his discoveries is an intact sunken pirate ship of the 1700's, loaded to the gunwales with a variety of loot—plates, jewels, coins—$40 million worth of treasure... Phillip Lief of the Phillip Lief Group brought Clifford to meet with eight publishers and spin them salty yarns of the pirate treasure, the Jolly Roger and the men who sailed under him. There was also a proposal.

After an auction in which six of the eight publishers participated, Clifford's book, *The Pirate Prince*, which he will write with Steve Kiesling, was acquired by Marilyn Abraham of Prentice Hall for $160,000 (not in gold). The manuscript is due next May, for publication in the fall of 1990.

—Publishers Weekly

On August 1, 1989, I stepped solo out of the twin-engine puddle jumper from La Guardia onto the tarmac of the Hyannis Airport on Cape Cod. I wore my *USA Rowing* cap, contact lenses, a polo shirt, shorts, and river runner's sandals. I felt expansive—as if I had been squeezed out of a tube. The clear blue sky was unframed. The breeze heralded ocean. I clasped my nylon duffel bag to my side, feeling the outline of a dive mask. What an assignment!

In front of the terminal Barry Clifford waited at curbside. Wearing his signature *Expedition Whydah* cap, a polo shirt, shorts, and Nike Cross Trainers, he leaned lightly against the side of a charcoal gray Saab Turbo convertible, top down. When he spotted me pushing through the glass doors, he gave a thumbs-up and slipped around to the driver's side. No spit, I noted. Maybe I had just imagined the white blob at the book packager's office. Now, under the white sun of August, Clifford's baseball cap didn't look ridiculous. Quite the contrary.

He started the engine while I tossed my duffel into the back seat and climbed in beside him. He popped a cassette into the deck, and we punched away from the curb with a squeal of tires.

"I didn't think it would be so successful," Clifford said as he negotiated the first roundabout, not giving way to anybody. "Jackie O had us for three hours at her cocktail party. At least one other publisher tied the winning bid, but Prentice Hall got the book because the editor is a diver." Clifford accelerated out of the roundabout. "She's coming to the Cape later in the month. Phillip Lief may be coming up too."

Clifford was now interested in the book business, wanting to know how our advance stacked up and how many copies it would take to make the best-seller list. I figured the advance was pretty good, and that we would need to sell about 40,000 copies.

"That's bullshit," he said. "We'll sell ten times that many."

Maybe we would.

Clifford was now fully occupied, weaving through the summer tourist traffic, so I read road signs and tried to remember what I'd learned about Cape Cod.

The Cape emerged some 15,000 years ago from gravel pushed ahead of two glaciers. It looked like an old anchor poking eastward into the Atlantic. One arm stretched north from what is now Orleans. The other arm stretched south from Chatham. But the southern arm has eroded away. Breakers crashing on a remnant of that arm forced the *Mayflower* to set a course toward Plymouth rather than continuing toward the Hudson River. Now even that sandbar is gone. In geologic time, the Cape is slipping northward like an anchor through sand.

I picked up a newspaper from the floor of the Saab and learned that multimillion-dollar homes near Chatham were falling into the Atlantic. The owners claimed the erosion could not have been predicted and wanted the government to bail them out. I almost asked Clifford about it but remembered that his own house was on the water.

"I talked to an old friend of yours at the Smithsonian," I said. "The maritime curator Paul Johnston."

"Oh, not this again." Clifford frowned. "Whenever the press needs someone to dump on the project, they call Johnston. At first he said the treasure didn't exist. When we found it, it really pissed him off. We had a professor write a paper about our African jewelry. She came to us for her data, and Johnston still wanted to shut her down. I'm sure he gave you an earful."

I nodded. "Sure did." I told Clifford about my inquiry into

a Smithsonian exhibition: how the Director had seemed in favor of the idea and how Johnston had shut it down. I also told Clifford what Johnston said about the Boston Tea Party— the chests buried under the substation.

"Did you put one over on the *Boston Globe*?"

Clifford grinned. "Of course."

"How come?"

"I got the idea during Bush's campaign," Clifford said easily. "He kept talking about how much junk was in Boston Harbor, so I figured it might be worth something to take a look. Three hundred lead-lined tea crates were broken up. There must still be pieces spread around the Harbor. "

"Why tea chests?"

"To focus attention on Boston Harbor and on my company, Maritime Explorations. I got the permit, and now I can dig anytime I want. All I have to do is dig one hole, and I'll tip that town on its ass."

I cracked up.

Barry continued, enjoying himself.

"In college I kept a case of dynamite under my bed. Used it for boulder rolling. All you need to start a landslide is to get one boulder rolling."

We turned onto Route 6, the two-lane artery out toward Clifford's house in Orleans. Entering the highway, Clifford worked up through the gears until we were doing almost 90 miles an hour before we caught up with the traffic. Since there was no passing on this stretch, he settled back. I looked at him and smiled. What an adventure this was!

"How do you make a living as a writer?" he asked.

He knew the structure of my deal with the packager. That wasn't what he meant. Suddenly it seemed important that we start communicating on as many levels as possible, so I told him about my hero, T George Harris, and the glory days at *American Health.*

Born on a farm in Kentucky, Harris was probably meant to become a preacher, but he became instead an artillery scout during World War II. He worked behind the lines, earning his commission at the Battle of the Bulge. He then went to Yale, class of '49, and graduated as a reporter for *Time.* He covered the mob in Chicago, the Kennedy asassination in Dallas, and the race riots in Watts. He created *Psychology Today.*

When I met Harris, in 1981, he was starting *American Health* and offered me a job. We were convinced the world could be saved by jogging—doing everything we could to spread the word—and our circulation rocketed to nearly a million. But we were always overextended, looking for ways to generate cash. And so, when Harris asked me to get us into the homevideo business, I tagged a video offer onto a cover story that featured Jennifer doing an exercise program. Though designed for back pain, the exercises had a side benefit that allowed us to call them *Bellyshapers! Send $39.95 for the video. Allow six weeks for delivery.* Three hundred orders was all we needed to cover production costs; if we didn't get that many, we would return the money. Because Jennifer and I wrote, produced, and hosted the video, Harris gave me a big chunk of the profits.

"How many did you sell?" Clifford asked.

"About fifty thousand."

Clifford grunted appreciatively. "Why aren't you still in that business?"

I wasn't sure. What I told Clifford was: "That first tape did so well that Lorimar, the movie company that produced Jane Fonda's tapes, took over. The Hollywood execs said my system of developing tapes was unethical and unprofessional. They insisted we produce the videos before selling them.

Lorimar lost a few hundred grand and pulled the plug.

"After that I wrote an audiotape for Nike. They produced the tape but had no way to distribute it, and so they gave me the tape master to use for a free premium offer: *Send two dollars for postage and handling*. Since it was free, both *American Health* and *Good Housekeeping* offered it to their subscribers. I made eighty cents on each order—thirty thousand times."

Clifford grinned, and I figured we had established a common language: greed. I didn't tell him, however, that I suspected greed was a symptom of something much worse—or that I dropped out of that business because my instincts seemed destined to get me into trouble. I also didn't tell him that publisher of *American Health*, a ruthless young entrepreneur with a very rich father, had expanded his magazine empire through junk bonds until the bubble burst. George Harris, who had put his own money as well as his heart into *American Health*, would lose his life savings.

What I told Clifford was this: "I became a freelance writer because it's a lot more fun.

"So is treasure hunting," said Clifford. He smiled broadly.

Clifford told me how he had risked his neck to find the pirate treasure—only to be bankrupted by archaeologists and forced into the clutches of Wall Street. When E. F. Hutton raised the $6 million, they seized control of the excavation. They took all the fun out of treasure hunting, and now they too were pulling the plug. To finance this last season of diving, the Wall Streeters sold the 165-foot salvage ship *Maritime Explorer*. Clifford's divers were stuck wasting time and money in their old boat, the 65-foot *Vast Explorer*, until he could find new financing.

It was ridiculous, he said. Thanks to the archaeologists, less than 10% of the site had been excavated. By the time our book came out, however, he hoped to be in the mother lode.

"A big discovery to launch the book?" I asked.

"Could be," he said, grinning.

We exited the highway into Orleans and were soon winding through a maze of narrow streets lined with traditional clapboard and shingle houses. As we turned onto Tonsett Road out to the point on Nauset Inlet, Clifford grimaced.

"You'd figure this out soon enough ," he said. "The I.R.S. has a lien against my salary. I'm still afloat because of Seahawk. I bought their stock before the discovery of that galleon hit the *Times*. After that, the stock doubled, and I sold it."

"How much you make?"

"Fifty grand."

I whistled appreciatively.

From the front, Clifford's house appeared a small summer place with a short gravel driveway, a narrow entrance, and a bit of lawn. As we walked alongside to the rear, however, the house proved to have been enlarged with a grand, open design, boasting floor-to-ceiling windows and French doors. A deck was obviously intended to surround the rear of the house but had not yet been built. Beyond the deck space the yard dropped precipitously to a band of thick grass. Beyond that were the calm waters of Nauset Inlet, dotted with lobster pots and clam beds, and beyond that the Atlantic surf. Clifford said his dive crews motored past the house each day in Boston Whalers on their way out to the wreck.

"How much did this set you back?" I asked, admiring the view.

"Eight fifty. Probably couldn't get that much now."

"I hear ya."

The interior of the house was bright, open, and surprisingly understated and elegant. Most of the main level was a single L-shaped space, containing the kitchen, dining area, and living room. The walls and beamed ceiling were painted white, and the floor was bleached oak. In the kitchen a restaurant-grade gas range perched on its own tile floor. The refrigerator was a Sub Zero, and the cabinets were custom oak. The house was suitable for *Metropolitan Home,* but there was still work to be done. The Sub Zero lacked the wood panels that would cover the gray steel front. The multipaned cabinet doors lacked glass. The counters had bare plywood tops or no tops at all. In one area a bedspread hid the contents of the top drawers.

The dining area was delineated by a Persian rug under a long table of unfinished pine, where one could sit and look out over the lobster pots toward the Atlantic surf. What struck me, however, was the 1960 edition of John Potter's *The Treasure Diver's Guide,* which lay open on the table. The book proved to be a catalogue of booty, documenting when, where, and how various ships had gone down, as well as estimating the treasure aboard and the value of whatever salvage had been made. Passages were underlined or annotated in the margins.

"This any good?" I asked.

"It's the bible."

Clifford was busy getting drinks from the refrigerator, so I checked the index and flipped to the entry on the *Whydah.*

> Testimony by surviving pirates from both ships indicated that about $100,000 in gold and silver money was stored below decks...

I returned the book to the table.

In the living room was a marble fireplace with a fine wooden model of a sailing sloop over the mantle. The remainder of the space was dominated by twin white overstuffed sofas that faced each other across a marble coffee table. In the center of the table sat a bronze bell about eighteen inches high.

"The *Whydah* bell?" I asked.

Clifford gave me a sharp glance. "That came from the wreck of the *Agnes Marie*. Then he smiled, reflecting on that adventure. "I swam with it to the surface. One of the hardest things I ever did."

The bell probably weighed as much as an anvil.

Surrounding the bell were stacks of treasure books and magazines: everything from children's adventure stories to *National Geographic*s to a monograph on the wrecks of the 1715 Spanish treasure fleet that had lured Black Sam Bellamy to Florida. As I scanned the books, Clifford crouched on the edge of the white sofa. He put one elbow on his knees.

"I think I have some instincts into finding wrecks," he was saying. "I'm starting to feel it again. I find them by sitting over these old treasure books. Good wrecks are everywhere. I don't care if you're a triple Ph.D. If you don't have salvage instincts, you won't know where to go."

I looked at him closely, and he appeared to be serious.

Clifford pointed out a stack of thick red volumes, his logbooks from the *Whydah* search. He picked one up and thumbed through it wistfully. A bit of a torn page fluttered out, and he stopped to retrieve it. He explained that his young lover, Heidi, had ripped or blotted out passages about his former wife.

Clifford set down the log and began thumbing through a volume of color photographs by Joel Meyerowitz. Clifford handed me the book, opened to a picture of a woman in her late teens standing on the beach in a white bathing suit. It was a picture of innocence and budding sensuality. It was Heidi. Perfectly cast as the pirate's Maria Hallett, it was easy to picture Heidi braving the cliffs in a northeaster, calling out to Sam Bellamy's ship.

"She was the real treasure," Clifford said.

"So I see. Any more like her around?"

Clifford chuckled. He scrounged around under another pile of books and pulled out a more recent newspaper photo, a profile of Heidi bursting out of a smaller suit.

"The fit model for Calvin Klein underwear—size six." Clifford announced. "She used to drive the crew nuts. They were all trying for her."

The Saab, the beach house, the babe with the pedigreed butt. No wonder archaeologists hated him.

My tour continued through more French doors to a den. Every flat surface in the room—the table, the trunk, and much of the floor—lay submerged under architect's drawings. He said the house was now only half as big as he had planned to build with Heidi. They had broken up, but she had called recently. He might invite her for the weekend.

Upstairs the two bedrooms opened out onto a single balcony facing the water. I dropped my duffel onto one of the twin beds in the guest room, and we met again on the balcony. Clifford had a handful of pennies, and he flung them out toward the water.

"For luck," he said. "Maybe they'll grow."

That afternoon Clifford drove me to the Captain's house, where he and his corporation's officers had lived during their first dive season. He turned the Saab onto a narrow old street shaded by ancient maples, pulled off the road, and pointed through the trees at a grand old spooky-looking clapboard house set on a deep green lawn.

"This house was the only place I was shown by the real estate agent," he said, as he shut off the engine. "Exactly what I had pictured in my mind—as if forces were pulling me along." Clifford pointed beyond the house. "That marsh used to be called Jeremiah's Gutter. It cut all the way across the Cape from Massachusetts Bay to Nauset Inlet. When Southack sailed from Boston to salvage the wreck, storms kept him from coming around the tip of the Cape. But the spring tide was running, flooding this swamp. Southack poled a whaleboat right across here."

We got out of the car, ducked under the maple branches, and crossed the lawn. Nobody was home, so I peered through the window into a den filled with antiques. Clifford stayed a few feet back. He seemed nervous, which surprised me. I figured he was a long way down this particular path to worry about trespassing.

"The day I moved here, I was all by myself," Clifford said. "That was one of the strangest days I can remember."

I looked back, and his face was as bashful as a Boy Scout's. The story came out haltingly.

When Clifford moved into the Captain's house, he came on the ferry from Martha's Vineyard. He had left his wife and three kids. He had left his business, which he now said was pumping insulation into old houses. Before that day he was nobody, and now he was president of Maritime Explorations, Inc. Coming into port in Hyannis, he looked across at the Kennedy compound, knowing that one of them would be working for him.

Met by an old friend at the ferry terminal, Clifford opened the car door and smelled brownies. He was warned about the marijuana mixed into the batter, but had had no experience with drugs. Besides, this was a special day, and he was ravenous. He wolfed down the entire batch before being dropped at the Captain's house—and crossed the threshold feeling very strange. The walls began to undulate. Soon the floorboards swayed with the walls, so he sat on the floor. Rockers rocked. Doors slammed. Two words stuck with him from the hallucinations—words spoken to him by an old portrait on the wall. The ancient visage leaned out of the frame to demand "the truth."

Clifford wasn't worried about trespassing, I realized. He was afraid of ghosts.

"Southack's voice?" I asked.

"Hell, no!" answered Clifford "Bellamy's."

That evening we drove for dinner to the Land Ho, a trendy restaurant and bar in downtown Orleans, where the original dive crew had run a tab. When we arrived, a line blocked the door, and the interior was packed, but the hostess recognized Clifford and ushered us to a table. As we sat down, a young woman in a billowing tank top and no tan line stopped by our table for an autograph. Clifford told her that I had been on the Olympic team and didn't mention Moscow. She leaned over to get an autograph from me.

Dinner, however, proved awkward. Clifford didn't hear well in the crowd. He said he had damaged his ears while diving and used to wake up at night and find his pillow soaked with sea water. I wasn't sure whether to laugh or not.

I learned that Clifford was descended from a line of Marines. His grandpa fought with the Corps during World War I and tried to re-enlist when Barry's dad, Bob Clifford, joined up for World War II.

In the rural, working class town of Hanson, Massachusetts, Barry Clifford grew up fighting. He thought "studying was for fairies" and got the worst grades in the class. In high school he was president of SHREC, the South Hanson Rat Exterminating Club, which met at the dump. Under the supervision of the football coach, a former Marine, they attacked piles of rubbish with Molotov cocktails and picked off fleeing rats with .22 rifles. Afterward they practiced knife fighting with rubber hoses, a skill that came in handy at motorcycle bars in Brockton.

And yet Clifford endured a postgraduate year at a prep school in Maine, two years of junior college on the Purgatoire River in Southern Colorado, and two more years at Western State College in Gunnison, Colorado. All to avoid Viet Nam.

At Western State, Clifford said he raised a pet coyote. The town made him get rid of it, so he let it go in the woods. But the coyote came home. He'd have to kill it, he figured. So, to avoid having to bury the body, he strapped his pet with dynamite, lit the fuse, and ran. But the coyote ran after him. It jumped into his truck and blew up.

During summers Clifford said he worked on the Cape as a lifeguard. To get girls, he would buy a dead shark from a fisherman and then tie the carcass to a buoy. Later, when a pretty girl went swimming, he would call a shark alert and dive into the water with a knife between his teeth.

"Did you ever tell the girl?" I asked.

"Of course," Clifford said. "If I didn't, it would be lying."

And Clifford had scalped a hippie. It was his senior year, 1969. He'd been thrown off the football team for assaulting the coach and felt like a deserter. Then a ponytailed man made at pass at his girl in the Alamo Bar. Clifford tapped the hippie on the shoulder and broke his nose when he turned around. Clifford took out a knife and chopped off the ponytail. He tied the scalp to his motorcycle and roared off. That same year Clifford's girlfriend, Patsy, got pregnant. A Catholic, Clifford married her. He graduated from college with a degree in sociology and a suspended sentence for assault.

By the time Clifford and I returned to his beach house, my head was spinning. I went upstairs to sleep but couldn't. I slipped on shorts and walked out onto the balcony. Despite the calm waters of Nauset Inlet glowing in the moonlight, Clifford nagged at me. He was an asshole. But he was my asshole. And I was curious. It had something to do with war—dodging the draft and scalping a hippie in the Alamo Bar.

"Remember the Alamo!"

My great-great-great-grandfather, Sidney Sherman, yelled that first at the Battle of San Jacinto. He had come from Kentucky with his own private army: 18 men, flying what would become the first flag of the Republic of Texas. Sherman's band joined up with Sam Houston's army to fight the Mexicans under Santa Anna. After the massacre at the Alamo, Houston kept retreating. A friend of President Jackson, Houston hoped to lure the Mexicans into the maw of the U.S. Army, a battle that would have made Texas part of the Union. But Sherman got fed up. On the plains of San Jacinto, he held a pistol to Houston's head and said, "We fight here." Sherman led the cavalry charge. His flag is enshrined in the state legislature, and his battle cry is in *Bartlett's Familiar Quotations*. Houston got stuck with Houston.

I first heard the family version of Texas history when I was about six years old, in the summer of 1964. My great aunt took us to the San Jacinto Monument (more than 10 feet taller than the Washington Monument) to see my ancestor's uniform. A crowd was there, and somebody joked that there were more tourists that day than soldiers in the battle. The

Texas Army was less than a thousand men. We took the elevator to the top of the Monument, and I remember being lifted up to look out through a coin-operated telescope: flat nothing for miles and miles and miles. I asked my great aunt how the two tiny armies found each other. I didn't ask why they bothered to find each other in that vast and empty land. I didn't have to.

A child in the sixties, I grew up among children of the sixties. My parents took it seriously. They sent me to an alternative school, where kids went barefoot and Joan Baez sang for free beneath the oak trees. I would then go home and find a circle of grown-ups sitting cross-legged, passing a joint from hand to hand, discussing the War, the population explosion, and people who could bend spoons with their minds. My father went to Yale and then law school at the University of Texas. His first case was to probate his grandmother's will, and he didn't really have to work after that. He quit the law and got a degree in physics and a job at Lockheed. Radicalized by the '68 convention in Chicago, he quit the Satellite Test Center to devote himself first to Zero Population Growth. I remember seeing a ZPG display of a bowl of gruel and a cup of soy milk—my daily fair share of the planet's food supply—and thinking my fair share wasn't something I aspired to.

A Catholic from my mother's side, I felt guilty.

I was more confused by Viet Nam. John Wayne went with *The Green Berets*. Muhammad Ali went to jail. Where I grew up the young men didn't do either. They said the War was our national war machine justifying itself. I figured our national war machine stood between us and our fair share.

When I was about 12, my mother stopped making me go to church, because of the Pope's stand against birth control. A year or so later, my parents divorced. So did the parents of most of my friends. Meanwhile, in the basement, my brothers and I built black-powder rockets that typically blew up while my sister re-created ancient battles using plastic soldiers on the ping-pong table. I once bought an Earth Ball, a huge canvas-covered inflated sphere designed for "peace games" in which no one had to win. I took it to my public high school. Commandeered instantly, the ball got shoved down the crowded corridor, scattering kids like bowling pins. After that spectacle of broken teeth and blood, I joined the football team. My defining moment took place on the 50-yard line. To make first-string I had to knock Randy over the line two out of three times. The first time I lost—and tore up my hand on a loose rivet. The blood pouring out would stop the contest, I thought. But it didn't. And I lost again. I couldn't bear to lose so I smeared blood across my shoulder pads and vowed to hurt Randy so badly that I would be first-string. My coach said I became a man that day. I became a first-string football player.

I followed my sister to Yale, where she had already gotten her picture in *The New York Times*—stark naked, with Title IX across her chest, protesting the lack of a women's boathouse. A military historian, Jennie would go on to collect university degrees like bowling trophies: Yale, Oxford, Stanford, Harvard.

I went east looking for a field to die on. Or maybe a cross. Instead, I too learned to row. Since the late sixties, Yale oarsmen wearing long hair and uncertain smiles had been losing by horizons and time zones. But we started to win. With every victory, our stakes got higher. Success became the only hierarchy. Friendship, even identity, had to be proven on the water.

The light came on in Clifford's bedroom, and I quit the

balcony. I went downstairs to the living room, flipped on a light, and picked up the top volume from the stack of log books on the marble table. When I opened it, dismay was a small word for what I felt. Clifford had written in his log about as often as most people do. Most of the pages were blank. I was then startled by what I read from September 25, 1983 — toward the end of Clifford's first dive season:

> I've shifted gears. My plan now is to continue the search and assume a more positive stance publicly and time a press release to throw my competitors off balance that will also push the stalk issue over the edge...

Stalks and bonds?

I flipped back to an entry dated April 13:

> 12:00 AM: Jackie Onassis called. She said Doubleday was re-evaluating the book, that she would call. Also she said she would rather do the book than anything in the world.

My mood improved. For six years Clifford hadn't been able to sell the book. Then I came along and started a bidding war. I went back upstairs to bed, thinking I was one hell of a writer.

The Kink

1717 was known as the year of the Great Snow...
On Cape Cod the body of Reverend Samuel Treat
could not be buried for several days while his
congregation, mostly Indians, dug an arch through
a huge drift to get the corpse to its grave. Had he
lived a bit longer, The Reverend Treat might have
been writing Black Sam Bellamy's epitaph when he
penned "Thou must ere long go to the bottomless
pit. Hell hath enlarged herself, and is ready to receive
thee. There is room enough for thy entertainment."

—The log of archaeologist Edwin
Dethlefsen, Ph.D., 1983

Confident that I was lost, I turned the Saab from an alley
into a parking lot somewhere deep in an industrial park of
West Chatham. I checked my notebook. What was written
matched neither the warehouse in front of me nor the duplex

office to my right. Late, lost, and with lousy directions, I realized something liberating. I didn't give a damn.

Shutting off the stereo, I was struck by a ghastly whine sounding like a dentist's drill. I got out and followed the noise around some parked cars to an open bay of the warehouse. The source proved to be an air-powered drill, wielded by a college kid sprawled across a plastic chair with his feet propped up on a wooden wire spool. He wore a T-shirt, blue jeans, green plastic goggles, and a Walkman. He was scraping bark from an old log wrapped in wet burlap.

"Hey! You in there. Hello."

No response.

I waved my hand in front of his face. His head slid back like a glacier, and his eyes were frosty by the time they got to me. When I didn't go away, he switched off the Walkman and then the drill. About that moment I realized the log was a cannon barrel. Behind him, another two dozen cannons lay submerged in fiberglass tubs. Smaller tubs on steel racks contained cannonballs and hand grenades as well as dumbbell-shaped bar-shot. I had walked onto the gun deck of a pirate ship.

"Restricted area," he snapped. "Tours start over there." He pointed toward the duplex.

"I'm allergic to tours," I said, realizing as I said it that I didn't want the official tour. "Besides, I'm writing a book with Clifford." This made no impression, so I told him I had just got off an assignment for *Sports Illustrated*.

He considered this. "Can you get me a date with Paulina?"

"I might find some out-takes from the swimsuit issue. The ones where she wasn't wearing so much sand."

He grinned and held out his hand. "I'm Skip Weeks. I could take a few minutes."

Weeks' summer job was cleaning the thick encrustation, called concretion, from the cannons and other large artifacts. The cannon he was working on, about six feet long and weighing some 1.500 pounds, was coated with a flaky black film that on closer inspection still looked like bark. Underneath the black coating, the concretion was the color and consistency of rust. Barnacles were visible—layers of barnacles—as well as bits of blackened wood.

"See this?" Weeks pointed to a bump like the top of a mushroom protruding from the breach of the cannon. "I think this is the butt end of a pistol." He switched on the drill to probe the lump. Despite the ear-splitting whine, his work was delicate, taking away little more than a pencil eraser would. He switched off the drill. "You have to take this real slow," he said. "Otherwise, you could turn the gun into goo."

"How long will it take?"

"A few months maybe, on and off. If it *is* a pistol, the wood is probably okay, but the barrel might only be a hollow space in the concretion. We could use it as a mold to make a rubber model of the original."

"How much you think it's worth?"

He scowled as if I were an asshole from Manhattan. "How much ya got?"

Beginning to like Weeks, I smiled and changed the subject. "Tell me, how did this pistol get stuck to this cannon?"

Weeks smiled too and switched into professor mode. "Concretions form when iron is submerged for long periods in sea water. The salt water reacts with the iron, creating an electric field, called a galvanic field, that attracts other objects and gradually encases them in a shell of rust. A large chunk of iron like this cannon can trap and preserve a trove of smaller artifacts." Weeks pointed back into the warehouse where another cannon, almost fully "reduced," soaked in a tub. "On that cannon we found silver coins, pewter plates, bits of muskets, part of a sword, a crow bar, some rope, and some gold dust."

As Weeks finished speaking I poked at the cannon, scraping at the black stuff with my fingernail. It didn't budge.

"Careful!" he snapped. "Some of this stuff that looks like iron is like rotten wood. Poke your finger through, and I'll be in deep shit."

I pulled my hand back but not before giving the cannon a final, firmer poke. Sure enough, the metal gave a little under thumb pressure.

Weeks cringed.

"Why is this stuff soaking?" I asked innocently, drying my hand on my jeans. "It's just water, right?"

"Yeah," he answered. "That's right." Weeks was tiring of me, but he was more excited about what he knew—and so continued. "The iron is saturated with salt. If it dries out, the salts will crystallize and destroy the thing."

I nodded and then remembered something. "I heard you guys dried out the gunpowder inside one of these cannons and were able to to light it."

"Sure," Weeks answered, shaking his head. "And we used it to blow open Al Capone's vault."

"Oh," I said, "just wondering." The reason I asked was that Clifford made the claim to Walter Cronkite. Cronkite didn't call him on the story, and I half believed it. It wasn't like Clifford had said it to Geraldo.

"Most of the real work here gets done by these," Weeks continued, pointing out pairs of electric wires running into each tub. "Electricity loosens the top layer, and then we scrape it off with the air drill. All told, cleaning and stabilizing each cannon takes a couple of years."

"Why not just paint 'em?"

Weeks shook his head. "Sure, you can make them look real good, but they'll fall apart. The rot's inside."

True enough, I thought. "You going to fire 'em when you're done?"

"Be smarter to give it to your enemy and get him to shoot it back."

I laughed, and glanced at my watch. I was now very late for my official tour. Too bad. "Will you show me the rest of this place?"

"Sure," he said, finally. "Why not?"

Weeks opened the door to an adjacent bay of the warehouse and led me into what looked like a large photographic darkroom. In the center were long wooden troughs supporting trays brimming with pungent chemicals. Piles of wood and rope soaked in the trays.

"These baths remove salts from the most fragile stuff," said Weeks. "The wood and cloth and paper."

"Paper?"

"Parchment used for wadding inside a pistol barrel. It came out perfect."

Weeks pointed to a coffin-sized device with a Plexiglass door at one end. A freeze dryer. "MEI is one of the only conservation labs in the world to have its own. This thing costs fifteen grand."

In a smaller room off the main conservation bays, two draftsmen sat on stools making detailed diagrams of the artifacts. The most important objects—including a teapot, pewter plate, and several navigation dividers—were also photographed. I thumbed through the albums and realized that I had seen all of these artifacts in the newspapers. The same few artifacts had been trotted out again and again.

"I thought you had a hundred thousand artifacts?" I said, as we left the draftsmen and returned to the bay of trays.

"Maybe we do," Weeks replied, doubtfully. "Musket shot, pistol shot, grape shot, bar shot, chain-shot..."

I waved toward the trays of rotten rope and splintered wood. "Not to mention this bullshot."

Weeks recoiled as if I'd hit him. I really was being an ass. My older brother the archaeologist would love this stuff. So might my sister, the military-history professor. So would a lot of people. But Wall Street? Not likely. Clifford must have conned them into doing something noble. Why?

Weeks opened a door leading to the parking lot and pointed me toward the duplex. "I've got to get back to my cannon," he said.

By the time I crossed the parking lot, Weeks was back sprawled in his chair with his Walkman and his drill, totally absorbed. I envied his excitement. He was on a treasure hunt. When all the concretions were scraped off and the cannons were painted shiny black, they would look as impressive as the guns at Captain's Cove Clam Bar in Bridgeport, Connecticut.

The ground floor of MEI's duplex office had a sliding glass door, which was locked. I banged on it without result and then tried the wooden door to my right. Unlocked, it opened to stairs. I trotted up, opened another door and poked my head inside. A pale, reedlike fellow sat hunched over a computer terminal like a preying mantis over an aphid. I knocked on the wall, and he unfolded himself from his chair and came toward me, rubbing his hands together. He had big eyes behind bigger glasses.

"You the piratologist?" I asked, using a term from the local papers.

"I've been called worse," the thin man said. "And you must be the writer." I held up my notebook in agreement, and he held out a long and bony hand. "Ken Kinkor," he said.

I expected the hand to be moist. It wasn't. "Sorry I'm late."

"Don't worry about it. I was just getting ready to print some files from the PSB—the *Primary Source Bulletin*. Pretty soon we'll have every known reference to the *Whydah* in one document. Printing takes forever on this machine. Hang on until I get it going. Then I'll give you the tour."

Kinkor folded himself back into his chair, and I looked around. The place was built as a one-bedroom apartment. Kinkor's desk sat in the living room. The bedroom was Clifford's office. The door was open, so I stepped inside and found a work table buried under scrolls of paper. Curious, I unrolled a couple of what proved to be nautical charts. The third scroll, however, was a photograph of a monstrously muscled man astride a Harley-Davidson chopper. It could have been a recruiting poster for the Hell's Angels.

The rider looked like Barry Clifford, only bigger. It was Rob McClung, Aspen's former chief of police.

Back in the living room the printer began to whir, so I retraced my steps. Kinkor stood by the door to the stairs, tossing a pack of cigarettes from hand to hand, ready to leave. When I confessed to having toured the lab with Weeks, Kinkor stopped tossing the cigarettes and frowned. I was pissing off everybody that day. While that could be useful in investigative stories, this really wasn't supposed to be one of those. All my instincts were wrong.

Kinkor then suggested we talk outside on a small wooden deck off the dining area. I looked at the pack of cigarettes and figured that Clifford didn't let him smoke in the office. "Sure," I said.

As soon as we cleared the door, he lit a cigarette and inhaled noisily, holding the smoke deep. When he finally let go he fumbled again for the pack.

"Excuse me," he said, and offered.

I took one, let him light it with his disposable, took a deep drag without gagging, and hoisted my seat onto the wooden railing.

"How did you come to work here?" I asked, watching him through the smoke. He didn't look like he ate much. His teeth were stained with nicotine and coffee. His long bony hands quivered. And yet, with one hand on the deck rail and smoke trickling luxuriously from his long nose, this thin pale man seemed to grow larger.

"That's a long story," he answered.

I shrugged. "I've got a hundred thousand words to write."

Kinkor stubbed out his cigarette and shook another from the pack. "I was working at a telemarketing firm in Iowa and trying to finish a master's thesis on Paulgrave Williams, Sam Bellamy's partner. Then I read in the papers about Clifford's search for the *Whydah*. We had a one-way correspondence for almost three years before he offered me a job. I drove out in the fall of '86, and pretty soon newspapers here were calling me a piratologist." Kinkor leaned forward and rubbed his hands together. A transformation was taking place on the deck: his face seemed to fill out. His gestures became bold. His voice would carry to the masthead. "You know, when I was about five my aunt read *Treasure Island* aloud, and I never recovered."

Kinkor was joking, but not really. I remembered an entry from Clifford's log regarding Kinkor's arrival on the Cape:

> Kinkor's on his way to Barnstable jail for DWI
> on a traffic violation. It's funny. Kinkor who studies
> pirates ends up in the same jail 299 years later. He

got stopped by Jeremiah's Gutter on his first night
in town.

"Shouldn't you be wearing an earring?" I asked the piratologist.

Kinkor laughed. It wasn't a completely friendly laugh, but before that moment I wasn't sure he could.

"You know why pirates wore earrings?" he asked.

"Not a clue."

"If your body washed up on the beach, the earring paid for a Christian burial."

I finished my cigarette and passed on a second. I should invest in an earring myself.

"Why a thesis on Paulgrave Williams?" My tone wasn't nice like I intended. It was kind of disparaging.

"That's for *my* book," he snapped.

I should have taken his lab tour, I realized. But what the hell? If Kinkor wanted to play, we'd play.

"Come on," I said. "It's going to be hard enough to get people to care about Sam Bellamy, let alone his lieutenant."

Kinkor sniffed down his long nose. "You know the Free Prince speech? The speech Bellamy supposedly delivered to Captain Beer?"

"Sure." I answered, and began to recite—pleased with myself for remembering: "'I am a Free Prince, and I have as much right to make war on the whole world as he who has a hundred ships at sea, and an army of 100,000 in the field: and this my conscience tells me.' I understand it's the most famous pirate speech in history. What about it?"

"It was reported by Daniel Defoe in his *General History of the Pyrates*. Defoe, of course, is most famous for novels like *Robinson Crusoe*, but he was also a journalist who interviewed a lot of ex-pirates. His first volume on pirates was accurate and made a lot money, but the second volume was rushed out. It's really unreliable."

"And Defoe wrote about Bellamy in his second?"

The piratologist formed an O with his lips and popped out a smoke ring. "You got it," he said. "Bellamy was aboard the *Whydah,* and Williams was in a sloop. The two ships got separated somewhere off Virginia. We know that Williams captured Captain Beer. If you believe Defoe, Williams took Beer aboard the W*hydah,* where Bellamy delivered the speech. But Williams and Bellamy were a long way from each other. It's very unlikely that Bellamy ever met Captain Beer."

I winced, and Kinkor continued. The piratologist had found his range and took his time to heat the shot. "Williams was a goldsmith, an educated man whose father had been attorney general of Rhode Island. He wore a peruke, one of those curled white wigs of a gentleman. Williams' sloop was spotted over the *Whydah* just after the wreck. His pirate career spanned the entire Golden Age."

The piratologist blew another ring, and watched it. "Actually, the Free Prince speech is in line with Defoe's own politics. Defoe probably made it up. But if a pirate actually gave the speech, it was Williams."

Kinkor's smile was almost a snicker.

I digested this new information for a few moments. It struck me that I had been hired to write about the wrong pirate. Kinkor obviously thought as much. He seemed to think it was funny.

"Where did Black Bellamy come from?"

Kinkor snorted. "Black was a nineteenth-century nickname—probably invented for the tourist trade."

"Oh," I said. "Where did *Sam* Bellamy come from?"

"Defoe wrote that Bellamy had a wife and children in the

West of England. Again, we don't know."

"What about that fifteen-year old beauty, Maria Hallett? The witch of Wellfleet. She's a big story around here.

Kinkor sniffed again. "Folk tales."

"So Bellamy didn't drown for love?" I was talking to myself, but Kinkor heard me.

"Dear god," the piratologist replied, drawing out the words sarcastically. "For that matter, we don't even know for sure that he drowned."

"What!"

"Read the PSB," Kinkor replied, and grinned. "One of our possible Sam Bellamys got married after the wreck."

"No shit," I said, and sighed.

I was defeated and Kinkor knew it. "Well at least the pirates freed the slaves..." I said.

But Kinkor shook his head. "The reason the *Whydah* carried treasure is that the slaves had been sold."

"Which means..."

"Which means the Africans still aboard were making the return trip. They were what's called "Gromettoes"—English-speaking blacks who gathered slaves out of the bush and kept them in line all the way to the auction block."

"Oh," I said again. A ship of pimps.

My only instruction from the book packager was to find parallels between the life of the pirate and the life of the treasure hunter—perhaps to start alternate chapters of *The Pirate Prince* with excerpts from Clifford's log or the re-created log of Sam Bellamy. But both stories now appeared to be bullshit. I had been conned.

What a mess.

To change the subject, I asked the piratologist what had brought about the Golden Age of Pirates, from 1715 to 1725, and Kinkor gave me a brief lesson in the history and economics of piracy—while I looked for parallels.

In 1701, King Charles of Spain died childless and left his throne to Phillip of Angou, the grandson of Louis XIV of France. The alliance between France and Spain, the two great Catholic powers, threatened Protestant England. So the Brits went to war. Queen Anne's War (the War of Spanish Succession) proved long, expensive, and vastly unpopular. To dodge the navy press gangs, armed "recruiters" who kidnapped men from bars and brothels, merchant sailors burned their faces with sulfuric acid to create scars that looked like scurvy sores or threw fits and frothed like plague victims.

Queen Anne's War sounded to me like Viet Nam; and, like Viet Nam, it was fought for reasons other than those told to the troops. The Peace of Utrecht, in 1713, won for England the *Asciento*, the exclusive right to sell slaves to the Spanish colonies of the New World. Although the slave trade was extremely profitable for companies like the South Sea Company, the crews on slave ships fared almost as badly as their cargo. Slavers like the *Whydah* often sailed with doubled crews because so many died of disease on the African coast.

But peace also left 40,000 British Navy sailors out of work, and so they fought for jobs even on slavers. Then, in 1715, a hurricane wrecked the Spanish treasure fleet off Florida. The wealth of an empire was dashed on the coral, and every unemployed sailor who could headed for the wrecks. All but a very few of those treasure hunters went broke in the attempt, but it was just a short sail from Florida to the Bahamas, a maze of 2,000 cays and reefs—paradise for pirates.

The Caribbean pirates of the previous century, called Buccaneers, typically flew their nation's flags and sometimes fought alongside their Navy. Some Buccaneers, like William Morgan, were knighted for their plunder. But the pirates of the Golden Age were a new breed. Perhaps it was because of Queen Anne's War; or perhaps it was because England flip-flopped between Protestantism and Catholicism; or perhaps it was the Enclosure Acts, which forced peasant farmers off the land so the nobles could raise sheep; or perhaps it was the large surplus population of the age; or perhaps it was the opening of the New World: whatever the reasons, these new pirates were especially angry and disillusioned. They declared war against all of it. For flags they chose warning signs from the Black Plague—a black flag with a dancing skeleton, the dance death.

During the Golden Age, these new pirates raised intimidation to an art form. Blackbeard, the most famous pirate of the Golden Age, was a psychopath who would be recognized today as a marketing genius. Huge and hulking, he bristled with weapons like a porcupine. Three brace of pistols hung around his neck, a couple of cutlasses were slung on his belt, and daggers were concealed in his waist and boots. Blackbeard once lopped off the arm of one of his mates and shot off the kneecap of another. When asked why, he replied, "If I did not now and then kill one of my crew, they would forget who I am." When approaching a prize, Blackbeard took lengths of slow-match, threaded them under his black cap, and then ignited them. Standing on the quarterdeck with a cloud of saltpeter and brimstone billowing from his head, Blackbeard appeared like the Devil himself.

And yet as spectacularly evil and as daring as the pirates appeared to be, they fought remarkably few battles. In his career, Sam Bellamy captured 50 merchant ships and lost only two men in battle. When those two were killed, Bellamy broke off the engagement and sailed away. Other than the final, fatal storm, perhaps the most dangerous event to take place aboard the *Whydah* was the play, *Royal Pirate,* staged on the quarterdeck to a rum-inspired crew. When "Alexander the Great" declared that he would hang the "Royal Pirate," a drunken gunner tossed a grenade onto the stage, drew his cutlass, and led a charge. By the time the play was over, Alexander had lost an arm, the Royal Pirate had broken his leg, and one of the gunner's companions lay dead on the deck.

Even the notorious Blackbeard engaged in deadly games mostly with his own men. He rarely if ever exchanged broadsides with another ship. Why? Because real fighting was bad for business. Instead, pirates offered "golden lifeboats" to any merchant captain who gave up without a fight. When Sam Bellamy captured the *Whydah*, for example, he gave his old ship to her Captain, Lawrence Prince, as well as a share of the treasure. In his career, Captain Prince lost three or four ships to pirates, and he probably died wealthy and in bed.

And though the pirates of the Golden Age declared war on the entire world, the reason for their enormous success involved collusion by the Navy. At the beginning of the Golden Age, when pirates first became a problem, warships were hired to escort merchant vessels in convoys. Convoy duty was legal and moderately profitable. But then, looking for ways to reduce shipping costs, merchants convinced naval commanders to carry cargo inside their warships. This "inside trading" was illegal—a warship full of cargo wasn't about to chase pirates. But the practice was also wildly profitable—and naval commanders were outside the reach of the law. The warships could offer lower rates than merchant ships, and much better security. The result was higher unemployment among merchant seamen, more men driven to piracy, and naval commanders who made a fortune by looking the other way whenever pirates sailed by.

And though the pirates of the Golden Age declared themselves to be Robin Hood's men, the ships they plundered were owned by small merchants who couldn't afford protection. During the Golden Age, the rich got richer, the poor got poorer, and the overall reduction in trade bankrupted the colonies. It seemed not unlike the United States in the eighties.

On the deck rail at MEI's office my butt was getting sore. Kinkor had run out of cigarettes and appeared to deflate. It was time to quit. We were getting up to go inside when I asked Kinkor how much treasure the *Whydah* carried. His eyes went far away, as he gave what I gathered was a stock answer.

"At their trial in Boston, two of Bellamy's gang claimed that the treasure was twenty thousand to thirty thousand pounds in gold and silver. Another pirate claimed that the treasure got divided into 'fifty-pound bags, one for each man's share, there being one hundred and eighty men on board.' Together those statements might mean that the treasure weighed nine thousand pounds and was worth twenty thousand to thirty thousand pounds sterling."

"How many coins is that?"

"Figure one hundred and fifty thousand to two hundred and fifty thousand. That's proving to be a reasonable guess. About ten thousand coins have been brought up so far, and yet less than ten percent of the site has been excavated."

Kinkor's big eyes focused on me. "No," he said. "I have no idea what it's worth."

"How many cannons have been found?"

Kinkor leaned against the door, thinking. "We have twenty-seven in the lab. At one point the divers had tagged more than forty cannons on the site."

"Forty? I thought it was a twenty-eight-gun ship?"

"The extra cannons were probably stored in the hold. Some of the guns appear to be have been covered with tar, which would make sense if the pirates didn't want them to rust during storage."

The piratologist walked with me down the stairs and waited while I climbed into the Saab and started the engine. As I drove away I began to wonder. The *Whydah* had twenty-eight guns mounted. Clifford now had twenty-seven in his lab. Perhaps another dozen had been tagged on the site by the divers. And Cyprian Southack wrote: *"The Riches with the Guns will be Buried in the Sand."*

Clifford had found all the guns. How could he have excavated only ten percent of the site?

I thought again of Kinkor's parting words: "Be wary of men who dream with their eyes open."

True enough. If Clifford weren't such a dope, he might be dangerous.

Crying Coyote

I have been fighting off personal problems w/
Rob [McClung]. His ego was driving him crazy. I
found a tape he made w/ my recorder. It was
predictable except he didn't believe the treasure was
there. (He doesn't believe). I can't believe it, to put
up w/ all this just for the money, to live a lie. To tell
people you're after the treasure when you don't
believe it's there! I'm too pissed off to think about
it any longer. His tape was filled with hate, distrust,
misery. I don't think I can tolerate his attitude.

—The log of Barry Clifford,
New Year's Day, 1984

I next wanted to meet with Rob McClung, but Clifford
said the former police chief was somewhere off the coast of
Florida. Clifford either wasn't sure what his partner was looking for or he wasn't saying. I then called McClung's house in

Chatham to leave a message and ended up talking to his new wife, Mary Ellen. She invited me for dinner to meet another member of the gang from Western State College. I was surprised she didn't invite Clifford, but that didn't matter, because he called to invite himself. We drove over in his Saab.

I was expecting something on the scale of Clifford's beach house, but the McClungs lived in a single-story tract home on a small lot at least a mile from the water. Decorating the driveway were a Porsche and a BMW, but both cars were of an age where their only assured destination was the repair shop. The iron bell on the front deck proved to be from a Spanish mission along California's El Camino Real. The interior of the house was what real estate people call "cozy." Mary Ellen, a slender and charming brunette in her thirties, made her home feel comfortable, but the McClungs were just getting by.

Mary Ellen introduced John Reese, the classmate from Western State. An amiable fellow pulling his life together after a divorce, Reese wasn't overjoyed to see Clifford. There was little conversation in the living room and not much more when we sat down to eat. Annoyed, I applied myself to the bottle of red wine. What a waste of time.

Then I had an idea.

"Mary Ellen, did your husband ever tell you about their pet coyote?"

She looked blank. "I don't think so."

I winked at Clifford. His big blue eyes went opaque. "Great story!" I said. "Let me tell it." I started without waiting for a response.

As I described the obliteration by dynamite of the pet coyote, Mary Ellen smiled beatifically, the perfect hostess. Reese looked puzzled. Clifford looked scary enough to scalp somebody. When I finished, Reese burst out laughing at Clifford.

"I hadn't heard that one," Reese said.

Without a word, Clifford and I drove home to his beach house. Finally, as we stood on the lawn outside his door, he broke the silence. He apologized for the coyote story and promised no more lies. He held out his hand, and I took it. I suddenly felt sorry for him.

Once inside, he sat on the living-room sofa to read the paper, and I called my answering machine. My agent had left a message that the contract with Lief was finally ready to sign. Next was a call from my wife's agent. Gillette was casting rowers for a razor-blade commercial. I had gone to the audition, and now they wanted me for the callback. The next call was from Tim, who just wanted to talk. I returned the call, but he was out. My wife was asleep.

I went upstairs and set out gear for a trip to the wreck site the next day. Looking at the wet suit hanging beside my bed, I remembered nights before races in college when I hung up my racing shirt. I felt the ebb of disappointment. This book would be like so many of those races. We exaggerated the strength of our opponents—relishing the fear and exhilaration of the close contest to come—and then, 20 or 30 strokes into the race, we'd discover that our competition was not in the same league. By the finish line we'd be close to paddling. Smiling awkwardly, we'd take their shirts as trophies while quietly cursing them. Competition, from the Latin root *competitio,* means questioning together, striving together. One doesn't learn from weakness.

I would tell my agent that Clifford wasn't worth my time.

But my wet suit wasn't wet yet.

Besides, I didn't want to go home.

And so another plan took shape. Because I hadn't signed the contract with Lief, I could stay with the story a little longer

and then quit if I had to. Feeling safe, I went downstairs, returned with a six-pack of beer and stepped out onto the balcony to watch the moonlight on the water.

The best race of my life—the four-miler against Harvard
my junior year—also began with a wave of disappointment.
We took the lead immediately and pulled away—like all the
other races that year. But we didn't quite break them. We
foundered in rough water, raced even for a couple of miles,
and then... We shattered the course record and lost.

That's the kind of race one dreams of and the last kind one
wants. Had I seen such a contest developing with Clifford, I
might have pulled out.

A Mat of Mung

When my eyes cracked open the next morning, I felt around for my Rolex, swore at it, and got moving as fast as the residue of the last night would allow. I staggered onto the balcony. Bright sun, flat water, light breeze. A fine day for treasure hunting. I looked down the line of lobster buoys and imagined that the World Rowing Championships could be held here—just like in Bled, Yugoslavia, in '79.

A pair of gulls swooped down at me and laughed.

"Take a couple steps to your left." It was Clifford's voice. I hadn't looked to see if his bedroom door was open and didn't now. Clifford sounded bright and cheerful, and it made me sick. I took a couple of steps.

"See that old gull on the rock. Eleven o'clock, a hundred and fifty yards."

I grunted affirmatively.

As the tip of the rock exploded in shrapnel, the gull took off. I turned around. Just inside his bedroom, wearing a bathrobe and slippers, was Clifford. He fed another round into the .22 rifle cradled under his arm and slid the bolt closed.

"Top of the morning," he said, grinning. He put the rifle back to his shoulder, aimed to the right of my belly, and dislodged another gull from its perch.

I mumbled something appropriate for a guest and headed for the shower. I took it cold. It didn't help.

The plan for the day was to go to the wreck site. Thinking we were in a hurry to motor out with the dive crew, I pulled on shorts, sandals, and a T-shirt and then grabbed my wet suit and headed downstairs at just about free fall. Clifford, however, wanted to go out for breakfast. We drove to a diner where he got to talking about his first adventure in salvage.

"It was 1976," Clifford said after the waitress took our order. "I went to the Pilgrim Society, in Plymouth, to draw some chairs I wanted to copy and sell. I got into a conversation with the director of the museum. He told me about a wreck in Plymouth Harbor called the *General Arnold*—a privateer from the Revolutionary War."

I poured down my coffee and sat up straighter. I'd never heard of this wreck.

Clifford continued. "There's a history of the ship at the house, but I don't know how accurate it is. The guy who wrote it is a sheriff named Cahill, who was on the state board for underwater archaeology. He writes all kinds of wild stories. He'd like to be a treasure hunter himself."

"How did you find the wreck?"

"I chartered an airplane from an old navy pilot to fly me over the harbor. I put up the money, but it was on behalf of the Pilgrim Society. I spotted something from the air and then went out with a local fisherman. I found the wreck no problem, but as I dove down I got swept under some ice and couldn't get back up. I made it to shore on a compass bearing and was able to brace my feet against the bottom and break through. I filed for a permit, and then things got crazy. It was the first Revolutionary War privateer ever found—and the Bicentennial year. Reporters showed up from everywhere. The night we were supposed to report our findings to the town selectmen, the fisherman showed up blind drunk. Scared to death. Someone had shot at him to keep him quiet about the wreck."

I was still wondering why this first privateer was not on his resume. And yet something in Clifford's voice convinced me that this tale, or most of it, was true. Calling him on the exploding coyote had worked.

"You get the permit?" I asked.

"Yeah. For the Pilgrim Society. Then a guy named Sanderson claimed to have found it first." Clifford sat back in his chair and fiddled with his napkin. "You should check out Sanderson. He tried to buy Hitler's yacht and moor it next to the *Mayflower* as a tourist attraction. He even tried to screw me out of the *Whydah*. The blue-haired ladies of the Pilgrim Society were so terrified of what Sanderson might do that they abandoned the claim to the *Arnold*. I wanted to fight Sanderson in court, but it wasn't worth it."

The breakfast check came. Clifford paid it, and we left.

A few minutes later, overly caffeinated and stuffed with cheese omelet, I stepped onto the dock at Goose Hummock Marina on Nauset Inlet. A wooden dinghy was tied up at the end of the dock, and I rowed us out through the fleet of moored pleasure boats to a battered 25-foot Boston Whaler. As Clifford opened the pilot house and started the twin V-6 outboards,

I returned the dinghy. He picked me up at the dock. I was leaning against the back of the pilot house when he slammed the throttle levers forward.

The motors howled, the stern sank, and the boat tried to take off vertically like the old gull from the rock. I lunged for a knotted rope hanging from the roof of the pilot house, but Clifford wrenched the wheel. I missed and sprawled against a bulkhead. Clifford must not have noticed, because he wrenched the wheel back again, tossing me in the other direction before I caught the rope. I just hung on as he weaved in and out of the lobster buoys and clam beds. Approaching the breakers into the Atlantic, Clifford kept the throttle wide open. We jumped the first wave like a motorcycle hitting a ramp, landing with a sickening thud that threatened to buckle the Whaler. I leaned over the side, just in case, and noticed deep cracks through the fiberglass just behind the pilot's house. I looked back at Clifford. He leaned into the wheel with his feet spread wide. His grin was bigger than I'd ever seen it.

From a distance, the *Vast Explorer* looked like a fishing trawler. The salvage boat was 65-feet long and made of wood. Her hull, stern cabin, and wheel house were painted white with black trim. A black steel tower strung with cables for heavy lifting rose behind the wheelhouse. A black flag flew at the masthead.

Moored alongside the stern of the salvage boat was another Whaler of a more recent vintage. Clifford eased us in just forward of it, and I jumped aboard the *Vast*. Clifford followed. He stepped onto the side rail and stood poised with one foot on an equipment box and one hand on a halyard. This was his first visit of the season to the site, and he surveyed the scene like an admiral. On deck, however, the men greeted him with all the pomp and deference due a delivery boy arriving late with a cold pizza.

Clifford muttered hello to everyone and took off toward the wheelhouse. I stayed behind. To learn anything from these men, I would need to keep as far away from Clifford as possible.

"Send down a metal detector."

I looked around and realized that the voice had come from below, through a loudspeaker mounted just forward. Underwater communications! At least one diver was already submerged. Leaning against the rail was a second diver, a freckled fellow stepping into a dry suit. He had a familiar face.

"Something bite you?" I asked, staring at a jagged four-inch red badge on his chest.

"Ay-up. A mako. Off Kauai." The voice placed him. This fellow had opened Walter Cronkite's news special saying, "A lot of people think we're just here to pull up the treasure and get rich, but we're here to learn about history..." His name was Scotty Magoun. Looking nothing at all like the Ancient Mariner, Magoun was engaging nevertheless.

I opened my notebook, and a *Sports Illustrated* pass to Madison Square Garden fluttered onto the deck. I took my time picking up the press pass.

"Tell me about it," I said.

"Some fishermen were chumming, and the shark went into a frenzy." Magoun ran his index finger around the edge of the scar. "Bit me right through my wet suit. I pulled a tooth out of the neoprene and now wear it on my season pass at Vail." Magoun then pointed to a small circular indentation on the inside of his arm and a larger scar on the outside. Entry and exit wounds. "Got that by hiking too close to a marijuana plantation."

At that moment a slim, muscular fellow with a crew cut

and spectacles emerged from a storage locker with what looked like a portable vacuum cleaner. "Scotty!" he said. "Would you kindly get your ass in your dry suit and over the side. And take this metal detector with you."

"Aye aye, Mr. Murphy." Scotty Magoun pulled the dry suit over his various scars and was zipped up by Murphy. Todd Murphy I knew had been trained by the Special Forces. He was now MEI's director of operations.

After Scotty's dry suit came the umbilical, a combination airhose, safety cable, and communications line, which clipped to the suit. Finally came the mask. It covered Magoun's entire face and allowed him to breathe and to talk normally. Magoun climbed over the rail and down a ladder onto a metal dive platform at water level. Todd Murphy handed him the metal detector, and Magoun jumped feet first into the water. As Magoun swam downward, Murphy fed more of the umbilical over the side from a coil on the deck.

"Think another shark will get Mr. Magoun?" I asked.

Murphy looked puzzled, then grinned. "I don't think there are two sharks doing skin-cancer surgery."

"Oh," I said. "I get it. What about the holes in his arm?"

"Somebody shot him. You can be sure of that."

"Does Clifford dive?"

Murphy frowned. "What story are you writing?"

"I normally write for magazines that have fact checkers."

"Lotsaluck." Murphy said, as he paid out a bit more of the umbilical. "Clifford's been bragging about this book, but none of us believed it."

"It's real. So what about the diving?"

"Clifford dove a bit the first season, when we were on scuba. He doesn't know anything about this new stuff. The last time Clifford did a magazine cover I put him into the dry suit and dumped a bucket of water on his head. Except for the baseball cap, he looked like Captain Nemo."

"What about his ears?"

"Who knows? Clifford said he was bounce diving and forgot to equalize the pressure. One of the hard-hat divers heard him. 'Yeah,' he says. 'I know what you're talking about. Sometimes I forget to shit for ten days and then I explode.'"

Magoun's voice from below interrupted us. "It's ringing pretty hard here. The area I'm working is five feet in diameter. It's one object. I'm having problems getting down. Send ankle weights."

Murphy left me to tend the umbilical and went back into the storage locker to fetch the weights. When he returned, he clipped them to the cable and sent them down. Moments later, Magoun requested a probe, an aluminum rod about three feet long with duct tape for a handle. That too went down the umbilical.

"I can probe pretty deep without hitting anything," came Magoun's voice from below. "Might not be deep enough. Might want to try another blow."

The director of operations swore under his breath.

"What?" I asked.

Murphy shook his head. "I've got to get Reedy."

Another "blow" meant turning on the *Vast*'s twin diesels and putting the twin props in gear. The salvage boat wouldn't budge because of three large anchors, two in the stern and one in the bow. Instead, the prop-wash blasted downward to the sea bottom through two elbow-shaped segments of aluminum pipe known as prop-wash deflectors or "mailboxes."

The decision to blow rested with Rob Reedy, the field archaeologist. Reedy emerged from the cabin, ordered the divers to surface, and consulted his log. Reedy then told his assistant, a college kid, to pass the word to the Captain to run the engines at 1,500 RPM for 15 minutes. Moments later, I felt the deep rumble of the diesels. Off the stern the water boiled, and soon a slick of sand flowed away in the current. Given the vibrations and the sand slick, this seemed more like blowing tree stumps with dynamite than archaeology, but what did I know?

After the blow Magoun dove again and reported that the pit was three or four feet deeper, but he still couldn't see the object. Down again went the metal detector.

"Runs out about seven feet," Magoun said. "A foot wide in the middle, maybe four feet at the other end."

Murphy let out a stream of oaths.

"What is it?" I asked.

"A goddamn Danforth!"

"A what?"

Murphy shook his head and started to chuckle. "We once had a giant buoy out here that got blown off in a storm."

"We're chasing our anchor?"

"Yeah, probably." he said. "It's gonna be hard to find out for sure. The Danforth's designed to sink in sand. The more we blow, the deeper it'll go."

Reedy's young assistant smiled broadly. "Salvage or scam? You decide."

As the mailboxes were hauled in and a dredge called an airlift was deployed to suck more sand out of the pit, the afternoon went by. Meanwhile, I went forward to make a sandwich and found Clifford sprawled on a bunk with the brim of his cap over his eyes and his mouth open, sawing logs. Disgusted, I returned on deck and sat next to Rob Reedy, the field archaeologist. About 45, Reedy had a gut over the front of his belt and a bowie knife over the back. His face was shadowed by a white hat and a cloud as dark and gloomy as Eeyore's.

Liking him immediately, I asked him about the project.

"My last project, HMS *deBraak,* was a grade-A wreck," Reedy began, wistfully. "It sank in ninety feet of water, and the hull was preserved in mud. A real time capsule. We even found the kitchen sink. But this..." Reedy snorted. He pointed toward the breakers some fifteen hundred feet away. "The surf doesn't look like much now, but the violence of this piece of real estate is incredible. As we archaeologists say, this site is biased toward high-density material such as gold and cannons."

"You're telling me the site's been trashed?"

"You could say that," Reedy replied. "All the light materials—wood, ceramic and glass—got carried away by the current."

"Or blown away by the mailboxes?" I asked impertinently.

Reedy sighed. "True enough," he said. "There's no other way to dig through the sand. We just have to be as careful as we can."

"So what happened here?"

"The wreck? It must have been dramatic. Just before midnight the pirates spotted the breakers. They dropped an anchor to keep off shore, but as the tide dropped, the offshore swell got rougher and rougher. They couldn't ride it out, so they cut the anchor cable and sailed for the beach. She hit the bar sideways and rolled over. This ship was busted apart and spread all over the place in a storm that lasted four days."

"How deep is this stuff buried?"

"I'll show you," Reedy answered, taking my notebook. He began to draw. "There's twenty feet of coarse sand. Under the sand is a layer of cobble. Below the cobble is a layer of fine sand, and then, eventually, a base of hard clay. The *Whydah* artifacts are on top of the cobble at the bottom of the coarse sand."

"You mean there's no vertical stratigraphy on this site."

"That's correct."

"I talked to a predecessor of yours, Warren Riess. He says there was vertical stratigraphy. It seemed important to him."

Instead of answering, Reedy pointed forward. "See that buoy over there, the one off the bow?"

"Yeah."

"That, my friend, marks an eternal monument to Warren Riess and his vertical stratigraphy. It's a giant cookie-cutter—eight feet square and four feet high. Made of steel."

As he spoke, the dark cloud over Reedy slipped away. He smiled.

"I don't get it," I said.

"Neither did Riess. We find most of our artifacts with metal detectors and the magnetometer, and that clown goes and drops a few tons of modern steel right in the middle of the site. Go figure."

"Just what was this giant cookie cutter supposed to do?"

"To set up a grid—to divide the bottom into eight-foot squares like a land site. The divers would work inside the box, using the sides to make both horizontal and vertical measurements. It must have looked good on paper, but it's a soup of sand down there. At first the divers couldn't make it sink, and then it got stuck." Reedy chuckled. "Then one of our competitors dropped a dime to the Corps of Engineers."

"How come?"

"The thing was called a cofferdam, so the Corps thought we were going to drain the ocean—to make the site a real land site. You can't do that without a permit, so the Corps shut down the excavation. Most of the '85 dive season got lost waiting for the permit. It might not have come through at all except Ted Kennedy's office called a special meeting and told the Corps to get its head out of its ass."

Todd Murphy, the Special Forces soldier, had joined us. He leaned against the rail, chewing a toothpick and listening. "You want to know the worst of it?"

"By all means," I said.

"I guess this is declassified." Murphy twiddled the toothpick. "You've got to understand, we tried to do everything that bonehead told us. Each day we swam into that box and dug a few more inches and took dozens more measurements— doing our best to be accurate to the nearest centimeter." He frowned. "But the whole thing was stupid. It was just a test. We had already opened the pit and knew it contained one cannon. But there were lots of coins outside the box. The archaeologist told us to leave them."

"What did you do?"

"What anybody would do. The stuff was going to get washed away in the current, so we picked up all the coins we could find and tossed them into the cofferdam. Then we measured them to the nearest centimeter and brought 'em up. The cofferdam pit became the richest pit on the site."

Reedy scowled, and Murphy laughed. "Don't worry Rob. We don't do that shit anymore." Murphy straightened up. "We've gotta get out of here now to catch the tide through the inlet."

"Did you catch that anchor?" I asked him.

"Not yet."

The following day, Clifford stayed ashore, and I rode to the wreck with the crew. The morning slipped by without a significant discovery by me or by the divers. Everyone was bored, so I convinced Murphy to let me dive into the mysterious anchor pit. He outfitted me with a scuba tank and showed me how to breathe using the commercial mask. Another diver escorted me down. He stuck like a barnacle.

A rope tied to the stern rail ran down between the two mailboxes to a lead weight at the bottom of the pit, about 30 feet down. We followed the rope. Seaweed, known to the divers as "mung," swirled and surged in the current. I couldn't see the bottom until I was almost on it. Then it was like parachuting through clouds into the desert. What opened beneath us was an endless expanse of white sand.

The pit looked about 20 feet in diameter and resembled a meteor crater. I reached the bottom, let go of the rope and was swept by the current up the side of the berm. I grabbed for the sand but my hand merely dragged through until I got my body turned to swim against the flow. The sand proved so light and loose I could wiggle my hand down to my elbow. My companion demonstrated how to fan the sand gently to find artifacts. In my excitement, however, I fanned too hard and immersed myself in a hail storm of tiny beads. For about ten minutes I fanned for buried treasure but succeeded only in burying myself. By the time my companion gave me a thumbs-up to return to the ship, all I could think about was the infamous cofferdam. Precise measurements in this soup would be impossible—and meaningless. No wonder the divers played tricks on the archaeologists.

When I surfaced and climbed back on deck, the crew was visibly relieved. Todd Murphy had let me dive because I had brought some gear, but he almost stopped me at the rail. "I don't mean to be an asshole," one of the divers explained later, "but you put on your wet suit backwards."

By lunch time, we still hadn't caught the missing anchor, and so Reedy, the field archaeologist, decided to give up. The crew hoisted our three anchors, and the *Vast* motored to a new site. Once again the anchors were dropped and the mailboxes were deployed. I could barely contain my enthusiasm when the first diver went over the side. This pit might contain treasure.

Moments later the diver's voice came over the loudspeaker. I couldn't make it out, but Reedy went ballistic.

"Mat of mung!" Reedy exploded. *"Oh shit!"*

"What's that mean?"

"Means we've been screwed!" Reedy stomped forward, leaving me with the divers on the stern deck. They weren't saying anything, so I followed the field archaeologist. I found him in the bow with his knuckles clenched white around the steel railing. He looked ready to hurl himself overboard.

"What's going on?"

"Friggin-mung." He was still seething.

"What about it?"

"When you open a pit, mung settles to the bottom. When the pit refills with sand, the mung gets compressed. You can cut it with a knife and roll it up like turf."

"Why are we digging here then?"

"Because we haven't dug here before. At least I haven't dug here before, and I've got no record of anyone else digging here." The vein in Reedy's neck no longer throbbed, but his voice still crackled with rage. "This isn't the first time. Far from it. Back in the lab we have all kinds of artifacts we now call 'pre-archaeology' because we don't know where they came from. The area up north was all worked and there is absolutely no record. We went north following an artifact trail, and it was clear that the site had been worked before. We spent half a million dollars digging in areas that had already been dug."

No vertical stratigraphy. Now a mat of mung.

No wonder Clifford had found all the cannons. No wonder a black flag flew above the *Vast Explorer.* And no wonder the field archaeologist lived under a dark cloud.

I told Reedy that my book contract allowed me the right to do a *New Yorker* profile of Clifford, that I was used to writing for fact checkers, and that I wanted to know the truth. Reedy seemed to be wrestling with himself. Finally he offered to write a list of all the people associated with the *Whydah* project. If I talked to everyone on the list, he said, I would have a fair idea what happened.

Reedy did not have to tell me that story would be very different from the official version.

That evening, as I returned home to Manhattan, I did some wrestling of my own—wondering if I should sign Phillip Lief's contract. I couldn't write *The Pirate Prince* and then contradict myself in *The New Yorker.* But I couldn't drop the book and just do a magazine piece. That would get me sued. The solution was to quit, but that would mean losing the story.

Damn!

Then Phillip Lief phoned to say that Clifford had made a mistake: when Clifford sold the wreck to Hutton's investors, he sold his own story along with it. The Wall Streeters wanted to meet me as soon as possible.

Then my wife's agent phoned. Although I missed the callback, I still got booked for the Gillette commercial, which was shooting the next day in Manhattan.

The Best a Man Can Get

"I want you to take twenty strokes... *flat out!*" It was the director's voice, sounding just like a coach. I rotated my oar, dropping the blade into the Harlem River, and glanced toward the dock into the maw of a megaphone and the eye of a 35-millimeter movie camera. The other two eight-oared shells were lined up on either side of mine. The coxswains hurled time-honored insults as if this were the Eastern Sprints rather than 20 strokes for Gillette. The day had been overcast and even rained some, but now it looked like we might get a few minutes of sun before twilight. The orange light popping off the water would be dramatic.

I rubbed my chin.

"This is hardest race you've rowed in your life," the director continued, now talking to the three principal actors in my boat. The rest of them were extras. "When I say *Now!* I want you to throw your hands up in victory."

I planned to row the Harvard race, the varsity four-miler on the Thames in New London. The three hardest races of my life, and I struck out. Now, in front of the camera, I would win over and over until I won perfectly! The Harvard alums in the designated-loser shells would not only make this fun, but therapeutic.

I sat in the #7 seat of the eight-oared shell, pulling a portside oar. I patted the back of #8, the stroke, who pulled a starboard oar. *"Let's do it!"*

The stroke grunted. Not long out of Princeton and with a silver medal from the '88 Olympics, he was above all this.

I swiveled on my seat to face the #6 man, a blond with perfect curls who arrived at the boathouse on a cute little motor scooter. The third principal actor in the commercial, he was a professional model. Inside the boathouse, I had asked him what side he rowed on.

"Right," he answered.

The choice was port or starboard, so I figured he could row as well as I could scuba dive. Hoping to persuade him to hop back on his scooter and go home, I introduced him to some of the extras in the boat—telling him about the world medals they had won. The model went pale, but he stayed. One of us was going to get hurt.

"When the director says now," I said, "make damn sure your blade is out of the water before you let go of the handle."

He scowled.

"Sit ready!" came the coxswain's voice.

"Row!"

We dug in our oars and pulled. In moments all 2,000 pounds of shell, oars, and oarsmen accelerated to about 14 miles per hour. The sun broke through, and the spray off the blades matched the brilliance of the sunset. This was a fast boat, moving well, and I was in the final meters of the Harvard race, closing on the finish buoys, having completely forgotten that I might catch an oar handle in the kidneys.

"Now!" the director screamed through his megaphone.

"Uggghhhhhhhhhhhhhh!"

It was him, thank god.

Sprawled flat on his back, the model held his ribcage and moaned as if he'd lost a jousting match. He had let go of his oar in mid-stroke. The handle missed me and continued through its arc, carrying with it the momentum of the shell until it hit his chest like a lance.

He caught his breath, decided his ribs weren't broken, and sat up, suddenly coachable. As we turned the shells around to repeat the race, I showed him how to protect himself, and he started giving me advice.

"If you're not in the shot, you only get paid for today," he said. "Three sixty-six. That's it. But if you *are* in the shot, you get residuals: ninety bucks every time the commercial airs. You don't have to say anything or do anything. You only have to be recognizable for an instant."

I knew this stuff from my wife. "So?"

"So the camera is only on one of us in each race. That's a one-out-of-three chance."

"No shit, Sherlock."

"So when the camera's on you, I'll throw my arms around you. If the camera's on me, you throw yourself in my lap. We're both in the frame."

The light came on. "Just call me Watson," I said, and fell backward into his lap.

I relayed the plan to the silver medalist from Princeton, but he wasn't up for it. Maybe he was just too young. He didn't understand that none of this was real. And so for the next hour or so, the model and I were all over each other in the thrill of victory. I left the boathouse confident I was in the shot.

I could now sign the contract with Lief, I figured. If the project got out of hand, I could claim that I had been deceived and bail out. Gillette would repay the advance. In the meantime, they would want me to do a good job. According to Gillette, I was the best a man can get.

Off to See the Wizards

The commonest plea heard at any trial of pirates was that the accused had been forced. This plea was rarely allowed, for the courts knew that pirates rarely forced men unless they were technicians...like carpenters and surgeons. Sometimes seamen had enough foresight to manufacture stronger evidence. This usually happened when a number of men on a merchant ship decided among themselves that if they were boarded by pirates they would join them. When the time came, a spokesman of the little band told the pirate quartermaster which of the men were in the plot, and asked for them to be forced. The request was granted with much waving of cutlasses and brandishing of pistols...Then, if the 'forced' men were caught, they would have the chance of calling witnesses who honestly believed them to be innocent. This ruse often worked.

—Patrick Pringle, *Jolly Roger:*
The Story of the Great Age of Piracy

Before there was any mention of buying a lake house, my wife and I arranged to spend the last two weeks of August at a waterfront rental on the Jersey shore. There we took sailing lessons in a catamaran and found a concretion washed up on the beach. I finished my how-to book on rowing and persuaded the owner of the lake house to hold a mortgage. I called my brother at the U.S. Embassy in Athens and learned about the politics of archaeology.

Archeology was once divided into separate camps, as different as ancient Athens and Sparta—and typically at war. In the Athenian camp were classical archeologists. Following the histories of Homer and Herodotus, they dug up statues and temples that were then used to illustrate the texts. They filled reports with photos, and tourists flocked to their museums.

In the Spartan camp were Native American archaeologists and anthropologists. Lacking classic texts to guide them, they had to guess where to look and then guess about what they found. Their only certain data were their own measurements, and so their reports were filled with details of digging techniques and graphs of artifact distributions. Aware that even the most careful digging destroyed that database, they learned to dig as little as possible. Finding less, they felt holier.

Of course both camps had common ancestors—treasure hunters. And it was the threat of such barbarians that brought the two together. The result was "historical archaeology" or "New Archaeology." New Archaeologists use the techniques of anthropologists on sites where there is already a complete historical record. For a New Archaeologist, it wouldn't matter that the pirates' voyage was chronicled in letters, logs, and court documents—or that the wreck had been blended by raging surf in soupy sand: the site would have to be mapped to the nearest millimeter. Someday some scholar might make some sense of the data. In the meantime, they'd all have jobs.

I read the Code of Ethics and Standard of Performance for the New Archaeology, a document so noble and self-serving it could have been written for the American Bar Association.

And so, by the time my wife and I returned to Manhattan, part of me felt sorry for Clifford. The Revolutionary War privateer in Plymouth Harbor, *General Arnold,* had been stolen from him. Then the pirate project was nearly scuttled by a new archaeologist with a cofferdam. Archaeologists had wasted so much money that Clifford had been forced to sell both the wreck and his own life story to Wall Street.

That was one theory.

In any case, I was more than a little curious to meet the partners of Silver Screen: Roland Betts and Tom Bernstein. Clifford first advised me to wear plenty of garlic. Later he mused, "They swallowed the hook, and it's coming out their assholes."

On Broadway at the corner of East 22nd Street is a rounded, modern-looking office building that has a store on the ground floor that sells nothing but light bulbs, *Just Bulbs.* If my investment-banker friends had gone into retail marketing, *Just Bulbs* is what they might have aspired to. It's as pure as you can get in retail. The store doesn't sell fixtures. It sells light. Incandescent, florescent, halogen, neon. Genuine Broadway light. But on the top floor of the *Just Bulbs* building is a place that deals in things even more tantalizingly pure and ethereal. It's a Wall Street firm on Broadway—the Alpha and the Omega of Hollywood fantasies—Silver Screen Partners. The company doesn't write movies or shoot them or distribute them. Silver Screen makes the stuff that makes movies. More of it than any single company in the history of Hollywood.

I cleared security first on the ground floor, rode the elevator to the top, and was cleared again through an empty glass-walled space into the reception area. A young woman waited there, as delicious as Ben & Jerry's and just as cold. She made the call and scowled at me as I poked around. The broad white hallway toward the number crunchers was hung with scores of constellations pulled together by Silver Screen's partnerships: *Who Framed Roger Rabbit? Pretty Woman,* and *The Little Mermaid.* Against the far wall, rising above it all, a stairway switch-backed upward to the twin penthouse offices and roof deck of the two principal partners. Those two *owned* the stuff that dreams are made of. With George Bush, Jr., the President's eldest son, they owned a baseball team, the Texas Rangers, as well as the pirate ship. I half-expected to be summoned up the stairs by a booming electronic voice hiding a couple of small geezers.

I clicked my heels and was surprised.

The two men who came down the stairway together were younger than I expected and less formal. Roland Betts was Clifford's age and looked remarkably like Senator Bill Bradley. Tom Bernstein, in his late thirties, was a young Eisenhower with red hair and freckles. They appeared pleased to see me. The feeling was mutual.

We shook hands and made our way to a conference room overlooking Broadway—establishing connections all the way. We were all from Yale. Tom Bernstein and I had the same history professor. Roland Betts, a varsity hockey star, had been elected to the same senior Scholars of the House program. Betts not only knew my editor at *The New Yorker*; they had played hockey together at Yale.

As we waited for coffee to be brought in, Betts and I talked about hockey, and it struck me that he had an edge to him much like an NHL all-star that I had once interviewed. I figured that edge had served Betts well as a captain of Wall Street.

I also asked Betts about his Scholar of the House project and learned that he had chosen to study a public high school in Harlem. After graduating from Yale, class of '68, he taught at the same school. The choice surprised me. I didn't picture him as a former school teacher. Betts explained that he took the job to avoid Viet Nam, and he winced as he said it. The memory was somehow painful.

Betts went on to say that he taught for six years and then wrote a book about his experiences called *Acting Out*. At the end of his twenties, and with a family to support, Betts quit teaching for law school at Columbia. After a short stint in the entertainment division of a major law firm, Betts joined a movie finance company that had a novel idea: "to sell the asset before you create it." And, like me with my home videos, he got lucky. His company provided seed money for *Ghandi* and *The Killing Fields*, the account of the last American journalist to leave Cambodia and the massacres that followed. Then Betts created Silver Screen Partners. The key to his success was a system that made Hollywood risks palatable to Wall Street.

Tom Bernstein, class of '74, took a more traditional path to success. He stayed in New Haven for law school and spent a year clerking for a liberal judge in Brooklyn, before accepting a job at the same law firm as Betts. By coincidence, they shared an office at the law firm and got to know each other before a glass partition separated them. Though younger than Betts, Bernstein was senior within the firm, so he took the side of the office with the window. When Betts left the firm for the movie business, it took a couple of years for him to persuade Bernstein to follow. Bernstein now considered Betts the smarter man because he spent less time working as a lawyer.

Tom Bernstein mentioned that his father was "in publishing," and I almost corrected him. The chairman of Random House and founder of Helsinki Watch, Robert Bernstein *was* publishing—or at least one of its principal power brokers. Robert Bernstein had connected Tom to Barry Clifford.

That meeting took place on the front porch of Robert Bernstein's house on Martha's Vineyard. It was August 1984. The *Whydah* cannons had just been located, and Clifford arrived at the house with a plastic pail of artifacts, hoping for a book deal. With Tom there, however, the conversation blossomed to include movies and a museum. Soon Clifford brought his pail of artifacts to New York for a dinner meeting with Betts. The Wall Streeters had to find Clifford a jacket and tie to get him into the restaurant, but the meeting went well. Afterward, they flew to the Cape and were taken on one of Clifford's wild rides through Nauset Inlet.

Betts chuckled at the recollection. "I threw out my back and became disoriented for two days."

I smiled back. "Clifford's driving is lot more dangerous than the diving."

"You dove?" Bernstein asked, surprised.

"Sure." I said, probably more surprised. It had never occurred to me that the Wall Streeters had *not* gone diving on the site. Why buy control of a wreck if you're not going to dive on it?

"You certified?" Betts asked.

"No. But it's only thirty feet deep. The only real danger is in-mung-dation."

"What?" It was Betts.

"The seaweed is called mung."

"Oh," said Betts. He wasn't interested in mung. "Just don't tell our insurance company."

Bernstein went on to say that they left the Cape impressed—and immediately formed a new company, Konkapot Partners, to market the *Whydah* story. Konkapot got *Parade* to do a cover story and Walter Cronkite to do a news special. Bernstein said their promotion work was as interesting a story as the tale of the wreck itself.

"So what's the story with Clifford and the book contract?" I asked eventually.

Bernstein pushed his chair back from the table and smiled. "We don't let him sign checks, if that's what you're asking. We don't let him do much of anything." His smile faded. "We have no illusions about Clifford. After the stock offering, when control of the excavation shifted here, I got a call from a Bruce Heafitz. A Harvard guy. You should check him out. Find out where his money comes from. Anyway, Heafitz started giving orders about how to run the excavation. I was taken aback, but not nearly so shocked as Heafitz would be." Bernstein chuckled. "He agreed to buy Clifford's stock in MEI for about eight million, and put up a big deposit. Heafitz thought he was buying control of the *Whydah*."

"Clifford fleeced him," said Betts, giving his knuckles a pop.

"So what about the book?" I asked again. It sounded like much the same story. Phillip Lief, the packager, and I had almost been fleeced.

"It's our book," said Bernstein. "We want you credited as the author. We can probably do that so long as Clifford's name is part of the title. We want you to verify whatever he tells you with at least one other source—preferably three."

"Don't get us wrong," said Betts, pushing away from the table. "I like Clifford a lot. We ski together, and he plays with my kids. But he lives in a different world from the rest of us."

"Can you do it?" Bernstein asked, also getting up.

"Sure." I said. "The field archaeologist is making me a list of all the people I should talk to."

"Good." Said Betts. There wasn't a trace of hesitation in his voice.

This was a more interesting game than I had imagined.

Before I left, I got a tour of the penthouses and was struck by an unfamiliar movie poster on Bernstein's wall: *Sakharov*. Looking closely I realized that Tom had produced the movie. Like his father, Tom was active in the human rights movement—the chairman of the International Lawyers' Committee on Human Rights. Through Bernstein's window, I then noticed a mural painted on a steam tower. Commissioned by Bernstein, the mural depicted the *Whydah* under full sail. Then Bernstein let it drop that he drove a Porsche, and it all made sense somehow. Bernstein started life with every conceivable advantage and had worked his balls off to stay on the right track. When he could afford it, he produced a movie that no one could ever fault him for. He bought a Porsche, a baseball team, and a pirate ship. It was easy to picture him strutting the cocktail circuit, dropping references to all his toys. Of course he didn't get his feet wet.

Roland Betts, however, was different. Athlete, author, entrepreneur. A Scholar of House from the class of '68. A true believer, he would stick his neck out. And he winced about Viet Nam.

A theory was beginning to take shape.

Betts was born to a bright new dawn after the Great Depression and the War to End All Wars. The country was the richest and most powerful the world had ever known, and its people paid the highest marginal tax rates to rebuild all that had been destroyed. Fueled by optimism, the birthrate rocketed upward, creating a generation unlike any other.

Baby Boomers were not conceived as investments. If they failed to prosper, a new safety net, Social Security, would catch their parents. Welfare would catch them. They were the flower of their parents' sacrifices, and every petal had to be perfect. Oddly enough the theories that nurtured these flower children came from a Yale oarsman and a gold medalist from the '24 Olympics, Dr. Benjamin Spock.

Their childhood was the time of John Wayne, close-knit families, and limitless dreams. Wealth replaced poverty. Unlimited education reached out to everyone. Penicillin took care of disease. A cure for cancer was just around the corner. A new advertising medium, television, taught them in 60-second mantras that they were special. Immortal. Then satellites poked into the heavens, and God wasn't there.

And yet the world faced a threat of Biblical proportions.

What was a young man to do?

In the winter of 1968, Roland Betts played hockey and finished his Scholar of the House project about a public school in Harlem. Hockey prepared him for battle. His senior project prepared him for a deferrable profession — teaching.

He had to choose.

While Betts considered his options in New Haven, in Saigon the Viet Cong overran the American Embassy during the Tet holidays. Scarier still were rumors trickling out about how Dr. Spock's new generation was conducting the war. A platoon of completely average young Americans led by an ordinary young lieutenant about the same age as Betts had lined up and murdered more than 400 unarmed men, women, and babies in a small hamlet called My Lai. The single American casualty was a soldier who had shot himself in the foot. They coined a phrase for soldiers who raped before they killed, "double veterans."

In the wake of Tet and just before My Lai, Walter Cronkite

went to Viet Nam to see for himself what was going on there. More popular than the President and with higher ratings than God (whose death had made the cover of *Time*), the anchorman concluded his broadcast by saying: "It is increasingly clear to this reporter that the only *rational* way out will be to negotiate, not as victors, but as an honorable people who lived up to their pledge to defend democracy, and did the best they could."

So the "best and brightest" of the Baby Boomers didn't have to follow John Wayne to war or even Muhammad Ali to jail. Betts chose to teach. In Harlem. To the younger siblings of those who couldn't afford deferments.

Betts had turned the other cheek.

Because all you need is love.

But he'd skipped the crucifixion.

One by one the heroes that Cronkite's *You Are There* introduced in the fifties were toppled in the seventies. The new teachers taught that Columbus was a scoundrel; that Jefferson slept with his slaves; and that the West was won with blankets infected with scarlet fever. Shortly after Betts quit teaching for Wall Street, Proposition 13, California's tax revolt, began the revolution that would gut the public schools.

And what about Silver Screen Partners? Was there a safe way to invest in Hollywood's fantasies? I could have saved myself a lot of grief if I had read *Forbes:*

> A whole new dimension in using other people's money…. About the only ones who don't make money are Silver Screen's investors. [fees to brokers brought in about $70 million.] And don't forget Roland Betts. He and Hutton control the managing partner which stands to make $34 million off the top over the life of the partner-ships, whether the movies did well or not. Now that's show business.

But I didn't read *Forbes*. And I didn't know that the title of Betts' book, *Acting Out,* means to throw a fit of violence. I only knew that at the height of the Golden Age of Corporate Raiders, Roland Betts reached out from his penthouse and seized control of the only pirate wreck from the Golden Age of Pirates.

And Betts winced about Viet Nam.

Here was a real story.

Before showing me to the door, Betts showed off the *Whydah* files in the main staff area. "It's all in there," he said. "You're welcome to it."

Suspended from the ceiling was a huge black flag with a skull and crossbones as well as the logos of Whydah Management and E.F. Hutton.

"That seems a little too honest," I said to Betts.

He clapped me on the back and smiled at the joke.

The Closest
Wreck to Wall Street

Just after midnight on September 12, I turned the Jeep onto Tonsett Road toward Clifford's house on Nauset Inlet. The mist hung thick as mung weed, and my wiper blades were shot, so I rolled down the window and shivered. On either side of the road, the summer cottages appeared empty. No cars lined the driveways. Tourist season was over.

At Clifford's house, no lights beckoned, and his Saab was not on the gravel drive. But another car faced outward in front of the garage—a gray touring coupe from the early sixties. A Jaguar. I got out and inspected the Jaguar and then peered through the garage window. Empty.

The side door of Clifford's house was unlocked as usual. Inside, nothing had changed in the month I was away. The face of the Sub Zero refrigerator still lacked its oak panels. The counters were still without tops. A bedspread still covered the uppermost drawers. I returned to the Jeep for my bags and carried them into the den. Something was making me nervous, so I set up my Macintosh and turned it on. The hum comforted me as I wrote notes describing the scene around me, warming up my brain for the days of research to come. The words came easily until I hit the Jaguar. Clifford was losing a chunk of his salary to an IRS lien. Whoever was building his house had apparently walked off the job. And yet he now had a Jaguar on display in front of his garage.

In his prime my grandfather would phone his boatman from Houston, kiss my grandmother good-bye, climb into his Jaguar, and scream off to his marina where the hooks would already be baited. A true Texan, he drank Dom Perignon from paper cups and once dinged the hood of the Jag on the landing gear of his buddy's Piper Cub. My father drove the car to Yale, where he was president of the sports-car club. He spent weekdays grinding valves in his room in Saybrook and then raced on weekends. I told Clifford all that when we admired a vintage Jag parked in Chatham. I even told him the money for the car and the marina and Yale came from an open field outside Houston that my great-grandfather bought for hunting ducks and later leased to Humble Oil, now Exxon.

I hadn't thought much of the conversation, but now...

If Clifford knew anything about Jaguars, he would never have bought this one: an orphan and a rusted one at that. The Jaguar was meant for me, I figured. A way of saying we were the same. But I didn't finish the story for Clifford. I didn't tell him that my grandfather's marina blew away in a hurricane, and while there was money left to build a new one, there wasn't the will. The Grandpoppy I knew stayed home in slippers drinking himself to death while bitching about conspicuous consumption and the theory of the leisure class. To get us to visit, my grandmother baited the Christmas tree with tens and twenties. I took to rowing with a vengeance because money couldn't buy it.

I didn't tell Clifford about the Mercedes either.

In college I promised myself that if I made the Olympic team and sold my Scholar of the House project to a publisher, I would use the advance to buy a vintage sixties Mercedes convertible with a four-speed. But when *The Shell Game* sold for six grand, I skipped the Mercedes, and inherited my grandparents' dump-runner, a dirt brown '74 Oldsmobile station wagon. The size of a hearse, it roared like a Harley-Davison. Everything on it was electric, and the electrical system had shorted. A bungie cord hooked over the dashboard held the accelerator pedal off the floorboards. And it was a blast: the ultimate beach car, with room enough for an Roman orgy. The car was also what I could afford on my salary from *American Health*—although the Oldsmobile came with enough cash that I could have lived like a school teacher for the rest of my life without a salary at all.

One my first real date with Jennifer I picked her up in the brown bomber at her parents' grand colonial in Darien. Both her parents came out. Her mother checked the car.

"What's this bungie cord?" she asked.

"You don't want to know," I answered. "But this car is the only one in the world long enough to carry a pair-oared shell to the Olympic trials. Then I'm going to take the car behind the barn and shoot it."

That was the right answer.

Jennifer and I then drove a couple miles to her grandmother's place on Contentment Island. Because my own family was spread around the globe, I was hungry for this closeness in Connecticut. The property wasn't bad either. For four dollars you can stroll through the Metropolitan Museum of Art and see the view in a painting by Kensett, but a million times that much wouldn't touch the house—the highest point on Connecticut's Gold Coast. Before it was grandma's, it was great-grandma's. In the driveway my brown bomber looked like a turd.

After losing the Olympic trials I told Jennifer my dream of buying a Mercedes. We were in a restaurant on Columbus Avenue when I described the model, the color, the four-speed. Then we walked out onto the avenue, and there it was: for sale. The owner, an Italian playboy, needed cash quick. The car had no seatbelts, almost no brakes, and steering like a prairie schooner. But it was beautiful. And she was even more beautiful in it. The perfect getaway car for the reception on Contentment Island.

Early on in my marriage, I felt bad about leaving my dead Mercedes to rot in my in-laws' garage. It really bugged them. The more I learned, however, the less I guilty I felt. Now it seemed the very least that I could do.

In Clifford's den, I turned off my computer and headed upstairs to bed feeling sorry for the treasure hunter. If the Jaguar was part of Clifford's game, he was losing badly.

The next morning the sky remained an impenetrable gray with a stiff breeze of 15 knots turning northwest. From the balcony I watched gulls flapping hard to stay in place. A dismal day for treasure hunting. Nevertheless, I grabbed my wetsuit and drove to the marina. Several of the crew were already there, sitting solitary in their cars. I recognized the field archaeologist and joined him beside his van. Now under real dark clouds, Rob Reedy looked more like Eeyore than ever. Bad weather had kept them on shore for the last 10 days, he said grumpily. Funds for the dive season were nearly exhausted.

Half an hour later, Todd Murphy, the former Special Forces

soldier and current director of operations, arrived from Marconi Beach looking glum. The swells were too big for diving, he announced. As the crew dispersed, grumbling about another day of reports and boat maintenance, I made plans to meet Reedy for lunch and then drove to McDonald's for coffee. Afterward, with nothing better to do, I returned to the marina, where two members of the dive crew, John Matel and Mark Enke, were adding yet another coat of plastic filler to cracks in the Boston Whalers. With bright red faces and sun-bleached hair, Matel and Enke looked like brothers—a result of the "Vail Shuttle." They skied all winter in Vail and dove all summer on the Cape.

"See there, where the hull is separating from the pilot's house?" said Enke, pointing to a crack in the Whaler. "Ads for Whalers claim they're unsinkable—even in three pieces. The question is, which piece do you want to be on when it breaks—the one with the engines or the pilot house?"

Enke slapped some filler into the crack and stood back to admire his work. "Fuckin-A," he said.

"How do you spell that?" I asked.

"I don't know. Fuckin-A. I guess."

"You want to go for a ride?" Matel asked. He was one of the few crewmen allowed to navigate the Whalers through Nauset Inlet.

"Fuckin-A," I said.

We climbed aboard, crammed ourselves into the pilot house, and within moments were at full throttle. "The faster you go, the less water you draw," Matel yelled above the outboards. "You hug the clam beds at thirty miles per hour."

"Matel is the Quahog kid," yelled Enke.

"Why?"

"Because he hugs the Quahog beds too tight sometimes."

Matel cut left, crossing close behind a cabin cruiser, jumping its wake. "Lobstermen call us yahoos."

"Why?"

"Because we *are* yahoos."

Enke explained that Clifford and McClung started the Yahoo tradition by racing the two Whalers home from the site. McClung's boat limped over the finish-line first, but Clifford tried to claim victory. He had done slightly less damage to his outboards.

Meanwhile, I was doing my best to look bored, hoping to goad the divers into wilder tales, the gorier the better. But the ruse wasn't necessary. Their stories poured out.

They told about the Wave a few years before, a wall of water higher than the *Vast Explorer*'s fly-bridge, that nearly scuttled her. Bags of groceries in the saloon were swept into the engine room. The radar was knocked out. Clifford made a big deal of the incident—about how brave he had been—which was kind of funny, because he wasn't aboard that day.

Another day a power inflator jammed, and the diver's dry suit suddenly filled with air. "I saw him shoot out of the water, fully inflated, a bloody mess," said Enke.

"Was he okay?"

"Sure," Enke replied. "Murphy got him into the decompression chamber, and it turned out fine. The guests on board didn't have a clue. They thought it was all part of the show."

Enke turned serious. "You want to know the most dangerous thing out here?"

I held up my pen, poised to write.

"Knocking Clifford's hat off." He burst out laughing. "Clifford was driving one of the investors out in an inflatable. He came through the break too fast, hit a wave, and flipped. His first words when he came up were 'Where's my hat?'"

"The first time I saw Clifford with his rug on was at a bar. I didn't recognize him at first. Once I regained my composure, I told him it looked good. I guess it did. I kind of hurt his feelings."

The divers fell silent as we completed the sweeping turn to the break in the inlet and discovered that the surf had calmed. Small ripples led toward a tranquil ocean. The sun came out. Too late we realized it had been a perfect day for diving.

It all seemed anticlimactic as we roared back over the clam beds toward the marina. This was Enke's final week with the company, and Matel was leaving soon. The fun was over. The previous summer they had brought up seven or eight cannons, more than a thousand coins, some gold jewelry, an anchor, a storage barrel, and the pelvic bone of a pirate. The current season wasn't so good: a .50 caliber machine-gun shell; a .223 caliber shell; a four-foot-long section of an air-to-ground missile; a sand fence lost during the 1984 season; two silver coins; and one piece of gold.

The gold caused the most excitement.

"We got a big reading with the metal detector and were really psyched," said Enke. "Then it turned out to be the sand fence. We spent a lot of time trying to lift the fence to see if anything was under it. We were about to quit when I found the gold."

"How big was it?" I asked.

"The size of a small booger," said Enke, breaking up again. "I brought it up and gave it to Reedy, the field archaeologist. 'You asshole,' he said. He had to log it in."

That afternoon at 12:30 I arrived at *La Cuchina,* a Chatham deli, for lunch with Reedy. I pulled into the dirt lot behind the shop and spotted the field archaeologist beside his van, gloomily kicking the ground with one boot. When I approached Reedy looked up and said ruefully, "This crew is united behind one thing."

"What's that?"

"Mutiny."

We entered the deli and got in line for sandwiches. He wanted me to know that he took diving seriously and archaeology very seriously. He had spent six years diving with the Navy and a dozen more as a commercial hard-hat diver and instructor. After all that he got his B.A. in anthropology. Now 45, he was completing his master's thesis.

I felt bad for Reedy but didn't let on. His previous shipwreck, the *deBraak,* had made *The New Yorker.* According to that story, several artifacts were salvaged without the knowledge of the state. When the state caught on, the salvor put them back:

> On the night of October 10th, they brought up the silver coins (now bright and shiny) for the second time... As for the ship's bell and the pewter chalice, they suddenly appeared on an inventory that was being kept by James Robert Reedy, a nautical archaeologist, who was on board the Mariner as the representative of the state of Delaware.
> ...Reedy was not, of course, deliberately misleading the court; rather he was testifying to when he saw the items for the first time, which, as things turned out, was when they were "discovered" for the second time.

In archaeological circles, that wreck became known as the *"deBraakle."* I figured Reedy took the *Whydah* job because he didn't have much choice. Maybe he had always been so gloomy, but I didn't think so.

We paid for our sandwiches, and I followed Reedy. A table

was free up front by the window, but he chose the empty room in back. "When I heard about the *Whydah*, I thought it was a state job," Reedy said once we sat down. "It wasn't until the end of the interview that I realized it wasn't. When I got here, I figured the project was financed out of Minneapolis. A guy from there would put big blocks of money into the bank in Hyannis, and Clifford would write checks. The company had money to buy a brand-new $25,000 Toyota Land Cruiser, but by Christmas they were eleven weeks behind in my pay."

Reedy started off slowly, talking between bites of sandwich. As he warmed up, however, he put down his lunch and began to dump on the project with a certain amount of glee. He smiled broadly when he told what happened once Hutton's money poured in.

"Once Clifford had big money, he needed a big boat. In Louisiana he found a monster. A 165-footer left over from the oil bust. It had a walk-in freezer, a walk-in refrigerator, a recreation room, state rooms, and bunks for a crew of seventeen. Clifford had it refitted with mailboxes, a fifteen-ton crane and two archaeology labs. It was renamed *Maritime Explorer*.

"The day before the new flagship was supposed to sail up here, an acetylene welding line leaked into the hold, and she got her nickname *Maritime Exploder*. It was miracle that nobody was killed. By late September, after another refit, she finally gets here. Clifford was strutting around like Captain Nemo until we realized that the *Maritime Explorer* and the *Whydah* had something in common."

"What's that?"

Reedy took a big bite of his sandwich and chewed slowly, savoring the moment. "A deep draft." he said. "Neither ship could sail close to Cape Cod at low tide."

"How could...?"

"When you're buying your penis, bigger is better."

Reedy chortled, and then sighed heavily. No matter how bad it gets, at some point you get to look back and laugh. Reedy was getting there. He shook his head and chuckled, letting go again.

"Get this! There were barnacles on the cannons!"

I waited. "So?"

"So barnacles don't grow on an artifact that's buried in sand."

Remembering the barnacles on the cannons at the lab, I slammed my palm against my forehead. *Stupid. Stupid. Stupid.*

Reedy continued: "Each layer of barnacles marks a different period of exposure—a time when the wreck lay open to salvage. Both sides of the anchor had barnacles, which meant it was turned over. We found dragger doors from a trawler underneath one of the cannons. A .50 caliber machine-gun shell was concreted to another. The idea of a zillion-dollar motherlode lying out there for 250 years is ridiculous, if you think about it."

"But how did Clifford raise so much money to keep looking for it?" I asked.

"It's a wonder, isn't it?"

I sighed. "This is going to be one hell of a book."

Reedy grimaced, gloomy again.

"What?" I asked. I had the feeling I didn't want to know.

"You know the story of Spider Savich and Claudine Longet, the ex-wife of Andy Williams?"

I knew that Savich was a skier. "Not really."

"Longet wasted Savich in Aspen. The murder weapon was confiscated and locked in the safe at the police department. The only people who had access to the safe were the police chief and the property officer. There were four court hearings. All of a sudden the murder weapon disappeared. Shortly thereafter, the chief resigned and left town. Claudine got a suspended sentence on a first-degree murder rap."

"You're talking about Rob McClung?"

"That's right. Whenever McClung needs money, he goes to Colorado."

"You think that's how this project got started?"

"Maybe."

I caught myself scanning through the open doorway to the tables in the front room. The deli was suddenly oppressive. "Let's get out of here."

"Want coffee?"

"Sure, but not here."

Later I would learn that McClung had nothing to do with Savich's murder or the weapon involved. But just prior to the treasure hunt, a .357 magnum pistol went missing from the property locker, and Chief McClung resigned under a cloud of suspicion. Rob Reedy's confusion may have been the result of a bump on the head he received when McClung decked him with a single punch aboard the infamous *Maritime Explorer.*

I followed Rob Reedy to his apartment, a dark and claustrophobic place on the second floor above a commercial establishment in Chatham. He lived alone, although he had a son who might be visiting soon. As the coffee perked, he identified the old rifles and bayonets displayed on the wall of his living room. Then he mentioned Clifford's wreck in the East River just upstream from Manhattan, a British Revolutionary warship called the *Hussar.* Reedy came late to the project, but was put in charge of archaeology. He said he had most of a file drawer filled with documents on the wreck, so we went into a back room to look. He opened the bottom drawer of the cabinet and began pulling out papers.

First was a front-pager from *The New York Times,* "1780 Gold Ship Reported Found in the East River," with a photo of Clifford and McClung watching the screen of a sidescan sonar, the same equipment used to find the *Titanic.* According to the *Times,* the *Hussar* had been carrying a British Army payroll, a pile of gold worth as much as $576 million.

> "We found it on the first pass," said the salvage expert, Barry L. Clifford, who had been looking for the *Hussar* for two years. "Just as I said 'This is where it is,' it popped up on the sonar screen...."
>
> The crew of the salvage ship spent four hours surveying the river between North Brother and South Brother Islands.... During the survey, Mr. Clifford said he found six other wrecks in the area "that were not the *Hussar.*"
>
> Mr. Clifford said of the shape, dimension, location and orientation of the wreck on the river bed that "I am convinced it is the *Hussar* because it coincides exactly with what my research findings had led me to expect."

The next clip was from the *New York Daily News.* Clifford told that reporter: "It is sitting there, pretty as a picture. You can't see a mark on the hull. There are no fractures."

As I read Reedy chuckled mirthlessly. "Clifford never went in the water, He was scared shitless — with good reason. It was a totally uncharted area in bad current. You couldn't see your hand in front of you. We had to crawl along the bottom."

"So what did you find?"

"The sidescan showed a hell of a lot of timber — which turned out to be old pilings. For two hundred years pilings had been dumped there. All of them coated with creosote. There were pockets of it on the bottom."

Reedy worked through the files again and pulled out a document barely held by an industrial staple. "Here. Take a gander at my report."

Reedy got up to check the coffee while I skimmed his report. Pockets of creosote were the least of their problems:

> There is no doubt that the remains of the *H.M.S. Hussar* lie on the bottom of the East River somewhere near the foot of 136th Street in the South Bronx. Documentary evidence to that fact is overwhelming. Due to a number of factors, primarily previous salvage attempts, the massive accumulation of cultural debris, and the natural deterioration of the ship, the physical evidence of her presence has been reduced to minimal proportions....
>
> An intensive research effort into the precise location of previous unsuccessful salvage attempts would be very beneficial to the current attempt to find the wreck. Likewise, detailed descriptions of the results of that earlier work would help the current salvors identify the remains when encountered.

When Reedy came back with cups, I held up his document. "You're telling me that three years after the discovery made the front page of the *Times,* Clifford decided to do some real research to see if the wreck was worth looking for?"

"That's about the size of it." Reedy handed me a cup.

"What did you find out?"

"That the wreck was stripped by a series of salvors. That the hull was dragged ashore, where it rotted away. And that the rest is buried under landfill."

"How much got spent on this goose chase?"

"Couple million maybe."

"Whose money?"

"Bruce Heafitz. He has an apartment in Manhattan over-looking the river. It was the closest wreck to Wall Street."

"Heafitz, huh?" I remembered the name. Heafitz was from Harvard. "I heard he got fleeced on the *Whydah*."

"Probably," Reedy replied. "He complained to the district attorney about the *Hussar*. They laughed at him."

So did we.

Before I left his apartment, Reedy gave me a copy of his report as well as a couple of other documents. Not sure what to do next, I drove to the strip of tourist shops in Chatham and parked in front of an antique store called the Spyglass. In the window were lovely brass telescopes and an oak captain's chest with brass fitting. I entered the store to read the price on the chest and learned that I could buy a rowing shell for the same amount. I picked up a pair of brass map dividers, and a clerk appeared.

"May I help you?"

"Maybe. You have any shipwreck memorabilia?"

"Certainly, sir."

"Coins?"

"Beauties."

He shuffled behind a glass display, brought out several silver coins in plastic holders. Spanish pieces of eight. According to the certificates, the coins had washed up on the beach from the wreck of the *Whydah*.

I admired them for a moment and began to gush. "These are in beautiful shape. Remarkably well preserved for beach coins. They look like museum pieces. I didn't realize you could buy coins from the *Whydah*."

"Four hundred dollars and that one's yours."

"Too steep for me at the moment," I said, handing them back. "What's that guy's name who found the wreck?"

"You mean Barry Clifford," the clerk answered. "He's a friend of the owner."

I thanked the clerk and walked out. As the door closed behind me, I muttered, "I'll bet he is."

After the Spyglass I drove back to Clifford's house. His bible, *The Treasure Diver's Guide,* sat prominently on the coffee table. I picked it up to check for the *Hussar* but was distracted by the newspaper photo of Heidi. She looked indeed like a fit model for Calvin Klein underwear.

I turned to the treasure book. Sure enough, the *Hussar* was listed: the first entry under "North American and East Coast Ghosts" in the chapter "Ghost Galleons and Treasures Already Salvaged." In the nearly page-long description, Clifford's bible had one word for the possibility of treasure aboard the *Hussar:*

"Inconceivable."

I replaced the book atop the photo of Heidi and ambled toward the French doors. The doors were supposed to lead onto a deck, and I imagined Heidi sunbathing just outside, her body spilling out of her white bathing suit. In the shelter of the house, she might skip the suit.

I checked the doorknob. Unlocked. The door opened into space. Step through and you'd break your back.

I closed the door, locked it, and forced myself to wonder about the *Hussar.* Why bother if treasure is inconceivable?

Of course! That Harvard man, Bruce Heafitz, had an apartment overlooking the East River. Perhaps he could step onto a terrace to watch his salvage boats go by.

Twice fleeced?

But Clifford's search for the *Hussar* did prove good for something. Almost. On December 18, 1988, *The New York Times* announced: "Salvager is Exploring Harbor for Boston Tea Party's Crates:"

> Although he has informal permission from state officials to scan areas of the harbor, he was turned down this month in his bid for exclusive rights to survey a nautical square mile. The State Board of Archaeological Resources told Mr. Clifford he must first retrieve artifacts from the site that are at least one hundred years old. He said he will renew his request after he finds some artifacts.

A month later, on January 27, 1989, Rob Reedy sent the following memo to various staff members at MEI.

> Re: Disappearance of artifacts
> and misrepresentation in official
> documents by Maritime personnel.
>
> On or about 18 January, 1989, two artifacts of possible major significance to the *H.M.S. Hussar* search project disappeared from their storage area on board *Maritime Explorer* while at her berth at SUNY Maritime College...
>
> Photographs of these two items, specifically a length of chain and a section of wood reportedly resembling the stem of a small boat, were subsequently faxed to the MEI office in Chatham for inclusion in our application for a permit to work in Boston Harbor. The artifacts were represented in this document as having been retrieved from the Fort Point Channel, Boston, during a dive conducted there on 16 December 1988. The artifacts themselves have not been seen since their disappearance from the hold of Maritime Explorer...

There was another thing to check. Reedy gave me a photocopy of log entry, dated October 5, 1986. The handwriting was Clifford's.

> I have never trusted either T. Bernstein or R. Betts—the Hutton deal which is now somewhat late leaves me ill—Having to listen to these snively nosed Yale Brats make me sick. I've had to leave Bucky [a lawyer] to handle talking w/ them as I can't bear to listen to more than a minute or two w/out getting serious impulses to spit in their faces.

I returned to the coffee table, picked up Clifford's 1986 logbook and opened it to the same date. The page was blank.

There was more than one log.

Barry Clifford: According to *Parade*, he is "The Man Who Found a $400 Million Pirate Treasure." According to Walter Cronkite, he did it through "intensive work in libraries and state archives."

But was any of this true?

According to the *Whydah* Media Plan — co-written by the chairman of Random House — "the media we will cooperate with in the months ahead will be carefully selected to provide us with print and television coverage that will, in words and pictures, tell the story that we want to tell."

Robert McClung: Was he telling the truth?

When McClung resigned as chief of Aspen's police department, the *Aspen Times* quoted the District Attorney saying: "The contents of a 30-page report prepared by the Colorado Bureau of Investigation made it clear that either McClung was lying or that everyone else in the department who spoke with investigators was not telling the truth."

Above: Bought with E.F. Hutton's money, this 165-foot salvage ship had something in common with the pirate ship: a deep draft. Like the *Whydah*, which wrecked just off the beach, the *Maritime Explorer* was too big to sail near Cape Cod at low tide.

Was Clifford's choice of flagship simply stupid—or diabolically stupid? (Photo by Stephen Rose)

Below: Under the layers of barnacles is a pirate's cannon, one of 27 in Clifford's lab. Finding the guns was critical because the big clue from 1717 read:"The Riches with the Guns will be Buried in the Sand."

But barnacles don't grow on buried cannons. Had the cannons—and therefore the treasure—been exposed?

Malevolent Forces

From the balcony the next morning, Nauset Inlet looked as flat and green as a pool table. The sun was bright, the sky clear, and hardly a breeze ruffled the lobster buoys. A perfect day for treasure hunting. I rushed downstairs hoping to be out the door before Clifford arose, but there he was—hatless! Impressively bald! Hunched over the dining table wearing a bathrobe, he looked like a monk at work on an illuminated manuscript. He ignored me, and I got close enough to see what he was writing on: *The Treasure Diver's Guide*. Knowing his page could be worth money, I figured, but I didn't stop to look. I just said good morning and gotta go. *What diabolically stupid scheme was he hatching now?*

At Goose Hummock Marina a few minutes later the mood was festive: conditions on the site were ideal. Joining a line of crewman, I grabbed a five-gallon gas can from the back of a pickup truck and carried it down to the dock where director of operations Todd Murphy was fueling the Whalers. Murphy and I had a couple of drinks together after my dive, and he was the most level-headed person among the dive crew. He'd taken ROTC in college and then joined the Army reserves, where he trained with the Special Forces as a medic. He stayed with the *Whydah* project because it was the best adventure he could get paid for—when he got paid for it.

I handed Murphy the gas can.

"Will the knucklehead be joining us this morning?" he asked.

"Nah. The knucklehead is doing research."

Murphy rolled his eyes. "Well, at least we'll get something done."

"What's the plan?"

Murphy screwed a spout onto the can and poured fuel as he explained the goal for the day: to locate a section of a ship's hull.

"We found the hull section back in '83, but the iron fasteners connecting the planks looked too modern. Now the guys at the lab say there are similar fasteners among the cannons." Murphy shrugged. "Who knows?"

"Think there's treasure under the hull?"

"Could be," he said. "We never did get underneath it. First we've got to find it again. Somewhere there's a notebook with Loran coordinates for the hull, but of course it's lost. We're gonna have to get out the magnetometer—just like the old days. It'll be good for your book."

Murphy was still pouring gas when a dark, unwashed BMW pulled into the marina's parking lot. The fellow who emerged was in his mid thirties. Tall, handsome, and dressed out of an L.L. Bean catalogue, he held a brown paper bag from which he brought out a liter of Japanese *sake*. He unscrewed the cap, took a swig, and held the bottle aloft, offering it to one and all.

"Who's that?" I asked Murphy.

"Charlie Burnham. One of the originals."

Murphy put down the gas can and started up the dock to shake hands with Burnham. I followed along.

"Mr. Kiesling," Burnham said before being introduced. His voice resonated with the irony of old Boston money. His eyes resonated with something else. One stared right at me. The other floated off. He held out his hand.

"Mr. Burnham."

"Class of eighty—if I remember correctly? You wrote a book?"

I nodded. "And you..."

"Class of seventy-six. Would you care for some *sake*?" He offered the bottle. "It's good, if a bit cold."

I shook my head. "Perhaps later." The scene had been lifted from a James Bond movie without Sean Connery. I hoped Burnham would cut the act before I had to. Maybe he wasn't acting? His floating eye made me uncomfortable.

"You were one of the originals?" I said.

"That I was. First investor, magnetometer repairman, video cameraman. Like Murphy here, I didn't get paid. Unlike him, I never expected to. I can talk to you."

Murphy grinned and turned away to get another gas can.

"So can Murphy." I told Burnham. "He says this stuff is declassified now."

"I'll be damned." Burnham took another swig of *sake,* screwed the cap on the bottle, and placed it on the dashboard of his BMW to warm in the sun. He gestured toward the Whaler. "Shall we?"

We walked back down the dock and climbed into the stern

of one of the Whalers. As Murphy started the outboards, I wrapped one arm through the loop of rope behind the pilot house and braced my legs. Meanwhile, Burnham plopped casually on the gunwale. He eyed me curiously as Murphy eased the Whaler away from the dock and out through the fleet of moored pleasure boats. Feeling a little foolish, I disentangled myself from the rope and joined Burnham on the gunwale.

"Not a bad commute," he said. "Smoother than the subway and infinitely more beautiful."

I agreed and for the next few minutes we played do-you-know games.

Burnham said that his ancestors were shipbuilders and whaling captains in Duxbury and New Bedford. Charlie prepped at Groton and then spent much of his Yale career on a Vermont sheep farm. His senior project was directing a film about "kids who came to Martha's Vineyard and decided to drop out of school and stay for the winter—about their disillusionment, drinking, and drugs." Now a producer of television commercials, he wintered in New York, summered on the Vineyard, and spent the shoulder seasons in Wellfleet. He still searched for the "quintessential New England experience" but feared that entailed moving to Maine, which entailed buying an airplane. The quintessential New England experience was not something one would want all the time.

As Murphy began the sweeping turn toward the break in the inlet, Burnham and I grabbed the ropes behind the pilot house. We needn't have bothered: Murphy had timed his approach so well that the Whaler entered the Atlantic with hardly a bump. When Murphy turned north toward the wreck, we sat down again and chatted until it was time to jump aboard the *Vast Explorer.* We got coffee from the galley and reemerged on deck to cursing.

"Youasshole!" It came out as a moan.

"Youheinousasshole!"

Draped over rail, the speaker appeared to have lost his breakfast. Beneath him, aboard the Whaler, another crewman stared upward, mouth agape and arms outstretched: the unmistakeable look of someone who tossed a thousand-dollar VHF radio not quite far enough. He lowered his head and peered down between the vessels into the depths. "Holy shit," he muttered.

From the stern deck Murphy rushed toward us. He grabbed a buoy, a Clorox bottle tied to a cinderblock, and tossed it over the side. "Suit up and find it!" he snapped.

The crewmen came out of shock and started to move.

"Nothing has changed, I see," Burnham said.

Murphy shook his head in disbelief and went aft again. I stood at the rail watching the Clorox bottle. "This proves a theory of mine."

"How's that?" Burnham asked.

"Well, this ship has three anchors out. It's not going anywhere. And that Clorox bottle is anchored by the cinderblock. But look. It's running like it's hooked to a tuna."

"Nothing holds in this sand and current."

"It's more than that. I rowed a pair in the '84 Olympic trials. That's a two-man boat—one oar each. In the first heat we had a really good start. But the five-hundred-meter buoy, a block of hard foam a lot bigger than that Clorox bottle, suddenly zoomed into our lane. Bam! We were dead in the water. We had a sports psychologist who claimed I was off the scale in distractibility, so my partner figured that I'd spaced out and run us off the course. But I knew the buoy had moved. I just couldn't prove it till now."

Burnham peered at me as if I might be as nuts as he pretended to be. This was good. "So what does all this mean?" he asked.

"It means there are malevolent forces at work here."

"You figured that out all by yourself?" He shook his head.

I let go of the rail. "Come on, let's go up front and get out of the way."

I ducked back into the galley to refill my coffee cup and grab a couple of doughnuts. When I came back out, Burnham waited on the foredeck. A private place, it was out of earshot from anywhere on the boat.

"What do you want to know?" he asked.

"Everything." I handed him a doughnut.

"In the beginning was the..."

"Fast forward to when you met Clifford."

Burnham leaned back against the rail and sipped his coffee. "It was at William Styron's house on Martha's Vineyard. About May, 1980. I was a good friend of the Styrons, especially his daughter Susanna. They adopt people every summer and Clifford was one of them. Styron thought we should meet because of our mutual interest in treasure. The two of us planned the thing together on napkins in Styron's kitchen. We figured the wreck would be visible to divers, and that the entire project would take a few weekends."

"What about Clifford's five years of research?"

"I guess that depends on your reading speed. We had two sources: a book of folk tales called *The Narrow Land* by Elizabeth Reynard, and a children's adventure book called *True Tales of Buried Treasure* by Edward Rowe Snow. There's a chapter in each. You can get them in the library."

This wasn't true, I knew. Such books are always missing. The first step in any treasure hunt is to clean out the public library.

Burnham said the project remained as napkin doodles until 1982, when a hypochondriacal crisis convinced Clifford it was now or never. "We realized we needed help," Burnham said. "A symbol to prove we were truly serious." And so in October they flew to Key West to meet Mel Fisher. Fisher's first big score, in the sixties, was the 1715 Spanish fleet. In 1982, he was coming to the glorious conclusion of a 17-year search for the mother lode of the *Atochia*. Much of what Clifford and Burnham knew about the father of American treasure hunting came from old *National Geographics*. They didn't realize that nowadays archaeologists blame Fisher for raping the wrecks of Florida. They construct Fisher dolls and stab at them with silver trowels.

While Burnham and Clifford waited for an audience with Fisher, they paid a few dollars to wander through his museum. There they handled a bar of gold through a hole in a Plexiglass display, and fantasized about finding their own. Such fantasies, Burnham noticed, could be profitable: coins available elsewhere for a few hundred dollars might cost a thousand dollars or more in Fisher's museum shop. The difference, I learned later, was Fisher's celebrity. When someone bought a coin at the gift shop, Fisher would amble out of his back office, shake hands with the buyer, and sign the certificate of authenticity.

Of course the great debate in any treasure hunt is the value of the Pile. Their first estimate, Burnham said, came from *True Tales of Buried Treasure*. Edward Snow valued Bellamy's treasure at a half-million dollars, but that was in 1947 when a silver piece of eight sold for about twenty-five bucks. Since Fisher's coins sold for more than a grand, the pirate treasure jumped initially to $15 million. Then Clifford and Fisher got together to discuss a partnership, and the Pile really began to grow.

130

In Fisher's experience with galleons, the actual treasure on a wreck might be twice whatever was registered on the manifest because contraband was smuggled aboard. He applied the same reasoning to the pirate ship. If the pirates testified in court that they had 20,000 pounds sterling aboard the *Whydah*, their actual treasure would be 40,000 pounds sterling. It didn't occur to Fisher that everything on a pirate ship was contraband.

Clifford's reasoning was simpler, said Burnham. Clifford read "twenty thousand pounds in silver and gold" as ten tons.

"He hadn't traveled much," explained Burnham.

By the time Clifford and Fisher finished negotiating their "Bellamy Contract," the Pile had reached $400 million—the value reported on the cover of *Parade*.

Much later I met Mel Fisher, and he gave me a copy of the Bellamy Contract. According to that document, Fisher owns 15% of the *Whydah*. When I asked Fisher why he didn't sue Clifford, the father of American treasure hunting smiled. "I've never sued anybody in my life. I've only sued shipwrecks."

At the stern of the *Vast Explorer* the two divers surfaced, and so Burnham and I wandered back to hear their report. The VHF radio was lost—as was one of their knives and a pair of Vuarnet sunglasses.

"Don't worry," one of the divers muttered as he hoisted himself back on deck. "We'll find this stuff next year."

Meanwhile, other crewmen were lashing a gas-powered generator to the roof of a Whaler.

"What's that for?" I asked.

"The magnetometer," Burnham replied. He pointed to a three-foot-long sausage lying on the Whaler's stern deck. "That's the mag head," he said. "We'll drag it on a cable behind the boat."

Burnham went on to explain that the mag head is full of kerosene—long, polarized molecules that behave like schools of fish. If left alone, the molecular schools align themselves with the earth's magnetic field. A chunk of ferrous metal such as a buried cannon creates an anomaly in the Earth's magnetism, and the molecules turn in predictable ways. At the other end of the cable the data was recorded in blue ink on a scroll of paper called a chart recorder. Whenever the mag head passed over an anomaly, the blue line lurched back and forth as if recording an earthquake.

Magging for the missing hull section was about to begin, so Burnham and I climbed aboard the foredeck of the Whaler. A small space without any rail, the deck sloped toward the water, and we had to stay low so as not to block the windshield. Nevertheless, we were out of the way, had an unobstructed view forward, and could talk without anyone else hearing. Looking back through the windshield, I could see Murphy in the pilot's house finishing preparations for the search. He started the engines and we motored nearer the surf line where the hull section lay. Burnham's story of finding the *Whydah* continued.

For the arrival of Mel Fisher on Cape Cod, on Friday, November 5, 1982, Burnham rented an unheated, two-bedroom summer cottage perched on a cliff in North Truro. He wouldn't tell the owners why he wanted the house, and they became "horribly suspicious" that a drug deal was going down. Their suspicions increased when Fisher showed up wearing a gold chain thick enough to secure a bicycle on the streets of New York. Then Fisher's associate, the magnetometer expert Fay Feild, started dragging in large boxes of electronic gear. The drama heightened further with the arrival from Brown University of John Kennedy, Jr. Meanwhile, Clifford had secured a lobster boat from a man known as Stretch, who got his nickname because he was six feet, nine inches tall, and because he did a stretch for smuggling dope.

Saturday morning, November 6, was bright, unusually calm, and so cold that Burnham worried that the water pipes would burst. While they waited for the lobster boat, the magnetometer expert went to the library to learn whether the Cape sand contained much iron ore, which might obscure the magnetic traces of the *Whydah's* cannons. Feild had no way of knowing, however, that sprinkled in the sand were things more contrary: bombs. A World War II gunnery range, the sand off Marconi Beach is spotted with dud ordnance and shrapnel.

Shortly after noon, the treasure hunters gathered at Chatham Harbor to sail for Marconi Beach. "Clifford was convinced by something that the wreck was right around the water tower," said Burnham. "We were excited and confident. Kennedy actually danced upon the engine cover." But though it was a great day for the New Englanders, the Floridians were freezing. Feild huddled against the wind, as he soldered loose connections on his home-built magnetometer. By the time they reached Marconi Beach and tossed the mag head into the water, Feild was miserable—and not thinking clearly. The treasure hunters were just beyond the breakers—over the outer bar, some 600 feet from shore. There they ran into a problem more vexing than bombs.

"Ah, the eternal cliffs," sighed Burnham.

Looking at the beach, it is easy to imagine Cyprian Southack on the same sand stepping over the bodies of drowned pirates. But the cliffs are retreating. And calculating the rate of retreat is not exactly rocket science. On the edge of the cliff directly opposite the wreck site are the foundations of two antenna towers from Guglielmo Marconi's radio station, built around the turn of this century to send the first transatlantic signal. A scale model beside the foundations shows there were once four antenna towers atop the cliff. Two have dropped into the ocean. There's even a white line on the model showing the cliff line in Marconi's time, and one can extrapolate from that to position the cliff line in Bellamy's time—two and a half football fields farther out to sea. To locate the *Whydah* where Clifford's team went magging that weekend, Bellamy's ship would have dumped her cannons on top of the cliff.

Nevertheless, the novice treasure hunters grew more and more excited with each new anomaly drawn on the chart recorder—and Fay Feild grew colder. Finally, Feild decided he wanted to go home to Florida. Directly opposite the Marconi model—and the two remaining foundations of the antenna towers—Feild looked at the pattern on the chart recorder, consulted his buoys, and declared a "cannon signature." Clifford donned scuba equipment, the only diving gear on board, and jumped over the side.

One version of that November dive was published in *Skin Diver* magazine. I figure it was the official version because the writer was Robert Cahill, a former sheriff of Salem and a member of the Massachusetts Board of Underwater Archaeological Resources:

> While scuba diving only 200 yards off the high sandy cliffs at Wellfleet, in fifteen feet of water, Clifford found a clay pipe stem, a handmade nail and two pieces of pottery. This was Clifford's happy day, for even though the articles he found were of little value he knew that buried deep under the sand were the remains of the pirate ship and the treasure she carried.

Burnham, who was on the cliff filming, surmised another scenario: "I knew that Clifford had worked a wreck on Martha's Vineyard and recovered some nails and pottery.

Knowing the only way to get a permit was to show artifacts, Clifford might have taken them down with him in his suit. Nobody ever questioned his production of those artifacts on that ten-minute dive. Wherever they came from, it wasn't the *Whydah* because she was buried under ten feet of sand and in a different area."

Later, when I phoned him at his home in Florida, Fay Feild mostly remembered being very cold that weekend. He didn't remember any artifacts being found. When asked about the "cannon signature," Feild replied, "There is quite an art to reading the results from the magnetometer..."Then he paused. "Well, not really. A 'signature' is a general way of talking that doesn't have a heck a of a lot of meaning. You've got to go out and check everything. There is so much man-made junk out in the sea. A wreck is just a little more junk. That's what's hard for a new person to understand. That's why Clifford was sure we found it."

When John Kennedy, Jr., finally returned my call, he was probably so stressed from failing the New York bar exam that he didn't even remember being aboard for the mag search that weekend. Regarding the project in general he said, "I was there. You can use my name. But I'd rather not talk about it. You understand."

On the deck of the Whaler, Burnham fell silent watching the cliff roll by. His face went melancholy. "I learned a hard lesson that fall," he said slowly. "I thought of myself as Clifford's partner. We shared the dream. I helped plan and pay for the venture. But Clifford didn't see it that way. He filed an Admiralty claim in his name only."

Burnham muttered something under his breath and threw up his hands, exasperated.

"So it goes," I said. But I too would have been pissed. Clifford assigned the salvage permit to MEI in exchange for

16 million shares of stock, about 40% of the company, as well as the promise of $150,000 in cash. Pretty good for a mag tape of the Marconi towers and some bits of junk from Martha's Vineyard. Then again, other companies have raised much more with less.

The next discovery happened the following August—immediately after Clifford got his permit to dig. By then MEI had raised a quarter of a million dollars in Colorado and bought the *Vast Explorer.*

"We found a piece of iron and decided it was a rudder strap to the *Whydah,*" said Burnham. "It kind of looked like a rudder strap. We also found a mizzen stay."

I had read about those artifacts in the clippings:

> "It's perfect," said Barry Clifford. "It's like a time capsule." Found was a 28' mizzen stay used to support the front mast of a ship and a rudder strap. He said he had studied the ship's plans for the *Whidah* which indicate that the mizzen stay for the ship would be 28 feet long and about seven inches in diameter. "That's exactly what we found."

Now I asked Burnham, "Did anybody really know what the *Whydah* looked like?"

"No," he said. "We still don't."

"So how did you figure out that you *hadn't* found parts of the *Whydah?*

"Because we visited the model of Marconi station. It was made of rudder straps and mizzen stays,"

Burnham broke into gales of laughter.

I stared at him in disbelief. Later, I would read Clifford's explanation in MEI's '83 Annual Report:

> A twenty-six foot 1" diameter iron rod was found
> from the tower. Interestingly, the *Whidah's* mizzen
> stay was a twenty-six foot long 7/8" diameter iron
> rod. We spent considerable time solving this mystery.

"We viewed ourselves as mercenaries in a sort of Adventure Theater," Burnham continued. "But Clifford was aware of the real situation. Investors were told they would own valuable treasure. The state was told we would build a museum. Cape Codders were told we would spend a lot of money and bring in tourists."

"Why didn't the press pick up on all this?"

"Clifford had a routine for dealing with reporters. He would drive too fast through Nauset Inlet, and they got wet. The wimpier the reporter, the scarier the ride. I don't get seasick, so I would eat sandwiches as reporters vomited over the rail. Female reporters were treated differently. The general effort was to get them into bathing suits."

"What about the archaeologists? That first guy was president of the Society for Historical Archaeology. Didn't he figure it out?"

Burnham reflected for a moment and sighed. "Ah, Dethlefsen. He was an older, tubby, ineffectual kind of guy who was always typing on a portable computer and making general pronouncements such as, 'It's not important what you find, it's what you find out.' We wrote a song about him. I can't remember how it starts... *I probe for gold with my aquaprobe, and someone is fucking my wife.*"

"What's an aquaprobe?" I didn't want to know about the rest.

"Oh that?" said Burnham. "Nothing really. The state worried that the mailboxes would destroy the site, so I created a piece of excavating equipment on paper that would be more gentle. It was a long tube with a pointed end that had holes for air to be blown through. I don't think it would have worked. But I showed the paper to Dethlefsen, who believed in the aquaprobe so completely that he wrote about it in his book.

"Eventually Clifford went too far. He decided to dig up the *White Squall,* a British wreck with a load of tin. We didn't have a permit for *White Squall.* It was probably in Matt Costa's permit area. Dethlefsen didn't know what we were doing until the divers started bringing up bits of a scupper. Then he freaked out. He was driven to the surf line and swam ashore."

Much later, from Clifford's log, I would learn that MEI continued to dig during that '83 season without an archaeologist aboard. When the state board complained, Clifford claimed that they weren't digging, just filming. Nevertheless, that first season ended as a disaster: no money, no crew, no lab, no office, and no *Whydah.* Even the press figured that out in articles like "Hard Times for Barry Clifford."

I also read more about how Clifford solved a final puzzle of his search. It happened the next season, on July 3, 1984. He had been lying in bed for hours when inspiration hit:

> The rudder strap we found is strictly inshore [of] where I think the wreck must be—we just did not allow for enough erosion.
> Nobody would.

Sure enough, Clifford's very first pits in 1983 turned out to have been directly in line with the wreck—just too close to shore. Except for the erosion, Clifford knew exactly where to go.

Aboard the Whaler that day with Burnham, I heard a shout from the stern and grew suddenly excited about our own search for the mysterious hull section. I leaped up and looked back over the pilot's house. But when I caught the eye of the archaeological assistant, he just shrugged. False alarm. So I sat back down. For some reason it didn't bother me that we were magging just beyond the breakers, only about 600 feet from shore. Treasure hunting must be contagious, because I was fully convinced that somehow we were going to find the legendary cask of East Indian jewels. Maybe I thought the pirates had buried them on top of the cliff.

In any case, another question had been troubling me.

The day of the actual discovery—July 19, 1984—NBC had a camera crew aboard the *Vast Explorer*. That didn't sound like a coincidence, so I asked Burnham how Clifford had set it up?

"He didn't," Burnham replied.

"Bullshit!"

"The NBC thing was real."

"Okay," I replied. "What happened?"

"Nancy Fernandez, the local stringer from NBC, was scheduled to come down. We didn't want them to film us *not* finding the *Whydah* again so we took her whale-watching. Afterward, there were two possibilities: we could dive on the hull section, or we could look further out and check a new pattern our magnetometer survey had found. The hull section was very photogenic. It looked like a shipwreck, and we knew we could find it. Clifford gambled on going farther out.

"McClung went down first," continued Burnham. "I was standing on the fantail with Clifford and Stretch, watching bubbles coming up between the mailboxes. 'God, he's breathing hard,' said Clifford. 'Those are *getting* bubbles,' said Stretch."

"Getting bubbles?" I asked.

"When you find something your breathing rate increases," Burnham replied. He continued: "McClung came up and reported two cannons in the bottom of the hole. Clifford and I concluded that he had found two large bombs. The NBC cameraman then dove with McClung, while Clifford and I ran back to the color monitor in the salon. We saw two black encrusted objects. *They were cannons!* The moment McClung surfaced with a cannonball there was a bolt of lightning. 'Ghostbusters' was blaring from the tape player.

"We didn't know what to do. The hole was open and anyone could come out and take stuff. It was raining and storming, and we had to pull the anchors to get the *Vast Explorer* to safety. Meanwhile, Clifford hammered at the cannonball and found a Spanish coin. We knew we had the wreck.

"It was the greatest achievement of my life. I had the intense feeling I could do anything I wanted. On my way back to New York to get my camera, I passed a note to a girl on the highway. We met in the city, had great sex, and then I never saw her again."

Burnham clasped his hands behind his head, closed his eyes and smiled broadly—perhaps reliving that great sex. I mumbled something about having to lose my coffee, got up, and slid around the pilot house to the stern deck, suddenly furious.

I hate feeling lied to.

Deep Doodoo

"NBC's camera crew was set up, weren't they? There's a story in this. I can feel it."

At the helm of the Whaler, Todd Murphy held his course and watched the thin blue line on the magnetometer's chart recorder. The Special Forces medic seemed to be making up his mind. Through the windshield, I could see Charlie Burnham, Clifford's first *Whydah* partner, still sprawled on the foredeck. Murphy must have watched our conversation. He saw us laughing, but he couldn't hear what we had been laughing about.

"What's Burnham been telling you?" Murphy asked.

"I'm not sure anymore. I saw the NBC tape of the discovery—if you can can call it that. I'd bet money the whole thing was set up as a publicity stunt."

"You'd lose." Murphy answered, still watching the chart

recorder. Nothing was showing up.

"So what did happen with NBC?"

"On the day of the discovery, NBC's cameraman happened to be aboard with an underwater camera. That footage was real. But the shots on deck were taken when we came back two days later with a different camera. Some people were kind of acting that day—as if the wreck had just been discovered."

"So it just *looked* like a hoax."

"If that's what you're looking for," Murphy replied. "Talk to Matt Costa, the guy with the black eye patch who owns the permit just north of us."

"Okay. What will he tell me?"

"Costa met us at Fisherman's Wharf in Provincetown when we brought in the first cannon. We were moving the gun from the boat to a pickup truck when Costa started screaming that we had salted the wreck. Costa was sure we had picked up the cannon either from Mel Fisher in Florida or from Rhode Island, where we did some salvage work. Then Costa started taking pictures. It was no big deal.

"Thing was, Clifford had sold the exclusive picture story to *Life* magazine, and the photographer was there. Clifford went nuts. He ripped the camera from Costa's neck and kicked it overboard. The crane operator, a friend of Costa's, decided to put the cannon back onto the boat. Before he could, Clifford cut the ropes and dropped the cannon into the pickup. We took off. Meanwhile, Costa went down to the corner drugstore and bought another camera. He started chasing us through Provincetown in a green Suburban—weaving in and out of traffic, taking pictures as he went."

"Murphy," I interjected. "Think carefully about what you say next. This car chase is very important to my screenplay."

"I'm not sure the movies are ready for this," he answered. "Clifford went to the cops and claimed that Costa opened his coat and revealed a pistol. He had Costa charged with assault with a deadly weapon and assault and battery. Clifford also said the cannon was encrusted with gold coins—making it out like Costa was trying to steal the cannon."

"Well, did Costa have a gun?"

Murphy shook his head. "I didn't see it. McClung got between Costa and Clifford to break up the fight, and he refused to testify. Said he wasn't going to lie under oath. Clifford *did* have a knife, and I heard him threaten to cut Costa's throat. But here's Costa, this swarthy fisherman wearing a black eye patch, telling the judge that the cannon isn't really a pirate cannon, and that Clifford's the real pirate. Then Costa brings out his pictures. They were taken at weird angles during the car chase. It was surreal."

"Who won?"

"Who do you think?" Murphy frowned.

"So Clifford lied under oath to convict Costa?"

Murphy didn't answer. He spun the wheel, turning the Whaler around to make another pass along the beach. Meanwhile, Charlie Burnham joined us from the foredeck. There was barely room inside the pilot house for two people, so he stood in the doorway. I felt much better about Burnham. I believed him again.

Murphy nodded to Burnham without taking his eyes off the chart recorder. "Do we tell our reporter friend about Disneyland?"

"Oh please do," I said.

"After you," said Burnham.

"No, you go ahead," Murphy replied.

"Shucks," said Burnham. He turned in the door to face

me. "You gotta understand something: We believed that when we found the wreck, money would pour in. Reporters like you showed up, but they didn't bring any money."

"Why would you need money once you found the treasure?"

"Get a grip man," said Burnham. "Treasure is very expensive stuff. Back then we had only a Reconnaissance Permit to *find* the treasure. Before we could bring it up, we had to establish the size of the site and the distribution of the artifacts. Then we had to create a Recovery Plan to get the Recovery Permit. All that takes an enormous amount of time and money."

Murphy cut in. "But at least we knew where the wreck was and could show investors a good time."

"Disneyland?"

"Yeah," Murphy replied. "Frank Wells, president of Walt Disney Productions..."

"Who got invited by the guys in New York, Bernstein and Betts, right?"

"That's right." Murphy replied. "McClung, Magoun, and I created an adventure just like Disneyland. We took a dive bag and filled it with artifacts we'd already brought up, and then hung the bag under the hull of the *Vast*. Before Wells was escorted to the bottom, we took the artifacts out of the bag and buried them in the pit." Murphy chuckled. "We wanted him to feel at home.

"I think it was Wells' son who found the gold ring," he continued. "The kid brings it up on deck, and Stretch says, 'Gee, what a coincidence. We found a ring like that yesterday.' The sad part was that Wells found a pair of brass map dividers and tried to open them underwater. They snapped in two."

"Where was your archaeologist?" I asked.

Murphy scratched his head. "I don't think we had one that day. In fact, I don't think we were even supposed to be digging. I'm pretty sure that was the summer of '85 when the Corps of Engineers shut us down because of the cofferdam."

Murphy looked at Burnham, and they both looked down at the deck. Maybe this stuff was more classified than they had intended?

But was it true?

Later I would find a clip from the *Cape Cod Times,* September 12, 1987:

> Wellfleet—The treasure must have been planted, thought Frank Wells, president of Walt Disney Productions Inc., when he first dived at the site of the sunken pirate ship, *Whydah,* coming up with handfuls of gold and silver.
>
> "I came up and I said, 'I don't believe you, Clifford. You're a fraud.' And I laughed," recalls Wells....
>
> Two years ago, each dive had produced a wealth of treasure. And Wells thought it had to be too good to be true.
>
> But he returned to Cape Cod a believer this time—and an investor as well. Someday Disney may even produce a movie about the pirate ship or a documentary on salvor Barry Clifford.
>
> "Every time we dived in a different location, we'd come up with more stuff," Wells said. "I realized how exciting and how real the treasure is...."
>
> Wells is one of hundreds of investors who collectively have contributed $6 million to the treasure hunt.

Still later I would I find two memos that dated from the summer of '85:

June 24
Kevin Wells,
Stanford CA

I enjoyed meeting you Friday night at dinner. As promised, enclosed is a copy of the *Parade* article on Barry Clifford. Let me know what you think.

Tom

July 2, 1985
To Frank Wells, President
Disney Productions

Barry is looking forward to spending the day with you and Kevin some time at the end of next week. His crew is assembled and should be diving by that time.

I have assembled an "interdisciplinary" package of *Whidah* material including historical, archaeological, and financial materials, as well as recent press clippings.

Sincerely,
Tom Bernstein

What Wells had witnessed sounded like Watts during the riots, and yet MEI's '85 Annual Report claimed that only two and a half test pits were excavated during that entire season— limited work because the Army Corps had blocked MEI from diving until September 5.

On the Whaler that day, however, I simply thought: no wonder the archaeologist now found unexpected mats of mung. More pits had been dug than the archaeologists knew about.

I wondered how many.

Except for the chugging of the outboard motors, things fell quiet on the Whaler. We cruised back and forth, riding easy swells, trailing the mag head, and watching the thin blue line. A few buoys had been dropped, but the whereabouts of the hull section remained a mystery. Finally, the archaeological assistant reeled in the mag head, and Murphy set a course toward the *Vast Explorer*. There the "shark-bit" diver Scotty Magoun confirmed the tale of Frank Wells' dive to Disneyland, but turned almost hostile. Out of earshot, Burnham explained that most of MEI's crew had never been allowed to talk to reporters. Magoun, however, often served as a company spokesman. I figured it was no accident that Magoun had been featured on Walter Cronkite's news special. I wondered if Magoun would report my questions back to Clifford.

The next morning Charlie Burnham stayed ashore, but the rest of the crew arrived early at the marina. By 10 o'clock we were on the site and ready to mag in earnest. Our job was to pick out the signature formed by the iron nails in the hull section from among the World War II bombs, bits of Marconi's tower, and the wreck of the *Castagna,* a 1914 cargo ship filled with guano for fertilizer. All of these objects, we figured, were buried under at least five feet of sand.

By 11 o'clock, the chart recorder on the mag was jumping. We circled the big hit and two more buoys were dropped. To pinpoint the location, the magnetometer head was brought to the bow of the Whaler and lowered straight down. Whatever it was, we were right on top of it.

By noon the *Vast Explorer* was moored over the site and the divers were in their orange and black drysuits. They danced on the deck like fire ants, getting limber, ready to go.

"Prepare for boxes away!" ordered Todd Murphy, the Special Forces medic.

The deckhands let loose the cables, and the giant tubes splashed over the stern. "Boxes away!"

"Diver in the water!"

The first diver carried a pneumatic gauge to record the depth before the blow. "Twenty-two feet on the pneumo" came his voice through the speaker on deck.

"Dropping the pounder!" called a deckhand. A lead weight on the end of a cable, the pounder marked the depth of the original sand. It got its name because it looked like a war club, and because various divers had pounded their heads on it.

"Prepare to start starboard engine!"

"Holy shit!"

The diver's voice was so full of wonder and excitement that everyone froze. "The cinderblock is sitting right in it. Looks like the fucking hull of a ship to me!"

Rob Reedy, the typically gloomy field archaeologist, grabbed the microphone. "Talk technical!" he ordered.

"All the framework is embalmed in concretions," said the diver in a slightly more controlled voice. "I see ribs, six inches thick and five or six feet long. Wait, this concretion looks like a swivel gun."

I nudged Reedy. "What's a swivel gun?"

"A portable cannon that swivels on a monopod—the pirates' favorite weapon. We haven't found any yet." Reedy's face glowed with excitement. "This is good. *Really good.*"

"Holy shit!" the diver said again. "*Infuckincredible.* You should see the lobsters. A shitload of lobster down here."

"Yeah, yeah," Reedy said impatiently.

"This thing is fuckin huge, concretion city. If the guys in

the lab could see this they'd have a shit... Wait!"

A long pause. "Oh boy..."

On deck nobody said anything. Swells lapped. Gulls cried.

"Looks like a bolt going into the sideplate of some kind of engine."

Another diver was hunched on the gunwale waiting to go over the side. "Please, don't let this be the *Castagna*," he said in a low, pained voice. But all of us knew that it was. We were atop what was left of 300 tons of bird shit.

Reedy went over the side to confirm the bad news. When he returned there was a short debate about what to do next. The reasoning went something like this: not enough daylight remained to locate and blow on another site; huge lobsters had been spotted; and the *Castagna* was too modern to be protected by state law. And so MEI's crew of dedicated archaeological divers armed themselves with pry bars and "bug" bags. Perhaps more excited than anyone, I pulled on my wetsuit and convinced Murphy to take me along.

Even in the surge of sand and mung, the site was breathtaking. Recent storms had uncovered the top of the hull, and we swam the length of her, poking into her hatches. I tugged with great enthusiasm but no success on one of the portholes, but others were successful with pry bars. They surfaced with several solid brass frames. The prize of the day, however, was a brass tripod about three feet tall with legs cast to look like serpents. Found in what was perhaps the Captain's cabin, it had supported a globe. Another round of debate ensued.

No one doubted that the tripod and the portholes legally belonged to MEI, which had funded the diving and owned the salvage permit. But there were other considerations. The lab staff would be furious that pry bars were used and no measurement were taken. The state might demand a special report. Perhaps worse, Clifford might display the artifacts in his living room and tell everybody that he had found them himself.

The diver who found the tripod then offered the most compelling argument—one that would cause the artifacts to simply disappear: "If we didn't know it was from a shipwreck," he reasoned, "we'd think it was a worthless piece of junk."

As we raced back toward Nauset Inlet to beat the tide, we talked about another trip to the *Castagna* for more souvenirs. The guano ship was only about 500 feet offshore and in only 22 feet of water. We could swim to it from the beach. We wouldn't even need scuba gear...

Then I started to laugh. The *Whydah* wrecked 600 feet from shore. Her cannons may have been buried quickly, but they had been exposed long enough and often enough to host layers of barnacles. Given our enthusiasm for diving into bird shit, I could barely imagine the fervor of those early Cape Codders in the weeks and months and years after the pirate ship hit the bar. That Clifford found any riches left among the guns seemed remarkable.

Maria's Curse
or *The Bald Truth*

The touch at the *Whydah* site is something to
consider. This has changed me. I wonder what the
ultimate change will be. You must risk everything
at least once in your life....

The log of Barry Clifford,
September 1, 1983

Sprawled across the day bed at the marriage therapist's
office, I looked at my wife with guilt and shame and thought
about things we should have talked about. Instead, she and I
killed the first part of our 50 minutes on insulation, the hard
foam kind we put in the loft of the lake house and the soft
pink stuff that filled gaps between the floor joists. Then we
talked about "captaining," something I was frequently accused
of. Captaining led to the "tit-for-tat," which led Peter to remind us that there are no "juries," and that we needed to act

as a "team." We didn't talk about sex, which wasn't surprising.

We were in therapy for what seemed a very long time before Peter got around to asking about sex. Of course I could have brought it up myself, but that would have meant admitting we needed therapy. So I waited till he asked. As I remember it went something like:

"Do you?"

"Not very often."

"Do you like it?"

"Yeah, a lot."

"Well, why don't you?"

"Don't know."

"Try it, okay?

"Okay."

The prescription had worked. Such a simple thing. And that success led to the question of babies. We were both in favor, we said. And we would go for it in earnest. Soon. But babies are a hard call for a model. I mumbled about wanting to hear one day that we were pregnant. Deciding to try and get pregnant, however, was more than I could do.

And then the prescription wore off. Rather than talk about why, I tried to get us away from the therapist. Peter countered that our marriage was too fragile to quit, too fragile to change therapists, too fragile even to risk confrontation outside the sessions. In the meantime, I came to dread therapy so much that we didn't talk there either. Peter said I was resisting. No shit. But what was I resisting?

In college once, on Halloween, I dressed up as a female hooker. It was safe, as such games go. I was at Harvard and was dressed identically to a couple of very attractive women, who talked me into the costume by promising to stay close.

But I remember looking in a mirror, checking the lipstick and eyeliner, and thinking that I appeared both feminine and vulnerable. The image threw me. Then I was asked to dance by a football player and was having a good time until I fell backward out of my heels and landed with my skirt up around my neck. I put the image from the mirror out of my mind. I wasn't trained to be a transvestite.

Over the years a couple of friends, including my old roommate Tim, had cracked open the closet door. Tim told me that his father, an extremely magnetic and successful man, had told him that there are certain things that every man feels — and that a gentleman doesn't act upon. And yet the further out Tim came, the happier he seemed. That made sense to me. If the core of your life is walled off behind bullshit, how can you trust yourself? After Yale Tim went off on wild jaunts to Morocco, where he could be anonymous and free.

When the pirate project came along, I read B.R. Burg's *Sodomy and the Pirate Tradition* and learned that men joined pirate gangs for sexual freedom. Pirate Articles typically forbade bringing women aboard, and some gangs permitted what amounted to marriage between men. For all we know, the *Whydah* was a twenty-eight-gun bathhouse—a notion that provided a new perspective on Clifford and his gang.

And then my oldest friend came to the lake house for a weekend, and we took a six of beer and paddled the canoe out into the middle of the lake. Greg was best man in my wedding. At that time, he too was on the verge of marriage to a pretty blonde. But they split up, and then Greg and I lost track of each other. Now, in the bow of the canoe, he turned to face me and explained that he had broken off his engagement to find out who he really was—and had never looked back. We paddled back to the house, and I hugged him, happy to know because we could be real friends again. Nevertheless, I was shaken. My marriage had gone cold, and two of my closest friends were gay. Maybe that old image of myself in the mirror was the truth?

I had no idea that what was really happening was the set-up for a monstrous and diabolical con. In this age of the plague, if my wife ever thought that I was gay, she would cut me off like gangrene—and her behavior would appear both inexplicable and vicious. But I didn't understand that. And I certainly wasn't going to tell either my wife or Peter about Heidi, the modern Maria Hallett.

At Clifford's house, I met Heidi, one of several young women who stayed there off and on. That day he was scheduled for knee surgery, and she came to escort him to the hospital. The three of us piled into his Saab. When we got to the hospital, Ken Kinkor, the piratologist, was waiting. He had gathered and filled out most of the necessary admittance forms and hovered protectively over Clifford as that job was completed. Kinkor didn't believe in the folk tales of Maria Hallett. He could find no genealogical record of a Hallett named Maria on the Cape in 1715—and he didn't care much for Heidi either. Kinkor left grudgingly as she and I escorted Clifford to the operating room. Clifford then tossed me the keys to his Saab and suggested I take her to Marconi Beach.

As a girl growing up in the pine forests of Truro, Heidi had taken up distance running. She moved like Nastassja Kinski in *Cat People*. Her brown, loosely curled hair was wild. Her lips were full. She wasn't 19 anymore, like when she met Clifford at a diner one summer breakfast. Now 26, she held pain down deep, but she still radiated an all-American vitality that, among other things, sells Newport cigarettes.

At Marconi Beach we kicked off our shoes and set off down the deserted sand toward the cliffs opposite the wreck site. As we walked just beyond the reach of the waves, she told me of her first date with Clifford: how he had scared the hell out of her in his Whaler and then left her at the wheel. She was a year out of high school then, and it was magical. They came to this beach not knowing for sure it was the *Whydah* site. He read to her from *The Narrow Land* about Black Sam Bellamy and Maria Hallett.

"I knew he was the one," she said.

Clifford took her to New York and to Vail. He took her out of college. She learned he had a wife and children on Martha's Vineyard, but she moved into the Captain's house nonetheless. He promised to get a divorce, but he didn't—not for years—and yet she stayed. She would wake up and find him at three in the morning, stark naked, hovered over his charts. "He was a little boy still trying to fulfill his big dream, with those little-boy ideals about life. 'I know it's here,' he'd say. I heard that a million times."

By then Heidi and I were opposite the orange buoy marking the wreck site, and she turned cartwheels in the sand to show how she had signaled to Clifford to come pick her up in a Whaler.

"It was magical," she said again.

We walked back to the car in silence, listening to the waves and the gulls. Afterward I saw her face each morning on the Newport poster at the corner deli on West 78th Street. Every so often I would see her whoosh by on the side of a bus.

Clifford said that Heidi was the real treasure—the one he'd lost.

I believed him. I was a fool.

Peter and my wife were looking at me expectantly. One of them had asked a question. I had no idea which. My wife's smile hardened. Her eyes froze over.

"Sorry!" I said, "I just figured it out."

"Figured what out?" my wife snapped.

"It's about pirates." I looked at Peter. He was into pirates. He had offered me a free session to talk about them. "How well do you know your mythology—the legends of the Crusader knights and the Holy Grail?"

My wife scowled, but Peter took the bait—and I stripped line as fast as possible.

"Start in 1150 A.D.," I said. "A young virgin, the bride of the Captain of the Knights Templar, dies on the eve of her wedding, and the grief-stricken Knight ravishes her corpse. Nine months later the Captain is summoned to her grave by a voice. He digs up her body and finds a living head between her crossed leg bones. He carries them at the front of his army. He becomes invincible."

Peter nodded sagely and scratched his beard, probably wondering if he had chomped on a rubber worm.

"Fast forward to 1717," I said. "The Captain of a ship flying a skull and crossbones—a flag of resurrection—returns to Cape Cod to collect his young beauty, but wrecks his ship on the beach. Maybe the Captain drowns? But maybe not?"

My wife glared at Peter, radiating exasperation. But he was still chewing the thing.

"Fast forward again to 1961. Barry Clifford is sixteen. He's rummaging through his mother's desk and finds a newspaper clipping from World War II saying that his mother was a war widow. Bob Clifford, the big Marine, isn't Barry's father." I paused, thinking about what that moment must have meant—how the pieces of Barry's life must have busted apart. "Barry was completely blown away. He still is. He took his hat off in public when he told me the story...

"So it's the bald truth."

"Oh please!" said my wife. But she was softening, and I kept going.

"Clifford told me that his real father was a pilot who got shot down over England. That's bullshit. I'm pretty sure that his mother's first husband, her high school sweetheart, was a soldier who died of disease before he left the States. She then moved to New York and immediately married somebody else. Somebody she decided was a swindler, out for her pension. She divorced the second guy."

My wife looked up, interested. Peter was almost incandescent.

"Here's the kicker: Barry was more than a year old when his mom married her third husband, Bob Clifford. Barry says he doesn't know for sure who his real father is, but he suspects the second guy."

"The swindler?" she asked.

"Yeah. Who knows if the guy was a swindler, but that's what Barry was told."

My wife smiled.

I had no idea what the smile meant. No way to know. She could conjure that smile on the worst day of her life. She met Clifford and immediately thought he was an asshole. She had no clue why I was interested in him. Maybe she smiled now because Clifford might be genetically an asshole. But she was smiling—and the session was almost over.

"Fast forward one last time to 1983. Clifford was high as a kite on hash brownies the day he moved into an old sea captain's house to start his treasure hunt. He was all by himself, having left his wife and kids on Martha's Vineyard. He heard a voice from an old portrait demanding 'the truth.' He thought it was the pirate talking to him."

Peter leaned back in his recliner and clasped his hands

behind his head, not saying anything. He left my wife to ask the obvious.

"So?"

"It's the fundamental mystery of the book, which nobody has been able to explain to me. Clifford got his salvage permit by using artifacts from Martha's Vineyard. He finally admitted that. But even so, he applied for his permit in exactly the right place. He just dug too close to shore. How did he know where it was? The question really bugs me."

As I said it I realized how much it did bother me. It wasn't fair somehow. "The guy didn't get much from his education and isn't much of a brain. So maybe the pirate talked to him directly. Maybe Barry Clifford actually *is* the reincarnation of Sam Bellamy."

"Wait a second!" It was Peter. "I thought your treasure hunter found a lot of ships."

I laughed—mostly at myself. "I have yet to find a single story that checks out completely. The most outrageous bit of bullshit was a wreck in Plymouth Harbor called the *General Arnold* that he found for the Pilgrim Society. Clifford told me that he almost drowned under ice while first diving on the wreck and that it was stolen from him by a man named Sanderson. But that's not what Clifford told Boston's Channel 4 News. I found the transcript. It's called *Piracy in Plymouth.*"

Peter and my wife laughed as well. I was going to make it.

"The wreck Clifford discovered was sticking out of the mud like a sore thumb. He got out of the boat and *walked* to it—and then announced that it was the *General Arnold*. He filed for a salvage permit on behalf of the Pilgrim Society, but then the director of the Society's museum did some actual research. The director found a letter from an owner of the *General Arnold* written after the ship went aground...

"The *General Arnold* was refloated!"

Peter leaned forward, "You're joking!"

"Nope," I sighed. "I should have known better. The ship was named after that great American turncoat, General Benedict Arnold. While the ship was being refitted for duty, General Arnold changed sides and joined the British Army, so the ship was renamed *Amsterdam*. Then the *Amsterdam* changed sides as well. Captured by the British, it was renamed *Maria* and sailed with the British Navy for ten years."

"So what *did* Clifford find?" Peter asked.

"The local fishermen always thought the wreck was a stone barge, and it probably was. But that didn't stop Sanderson. He still claimed it was the *General Arnold*. He called it 'priceless' and applied for a $5-million-dollar federal grant to excavate it.

"And get this! E.F. Hutton's offering was originally for $5 million dollars. The brokers' and lawyers' fees jacked it up to $6 million."

Peter exhaled loudly and sat back in his chair. "My, oh my," he said, as he rotated the recliner back and forth. "You're saying the pirate ship is a hoax?"

"Not exactly. The ship is real. I saw the bell. It has *Whydah* written on it. There's no way it could have been faked. Something else is going on. I've been on the salvage boat for a total of four days. The first two we chased our own anchor. After that we found and looted a wreck loaded with bird shit. They're pouring money into the ocean."

I was losing my audience, but it didn't matter. I was thinking instead of my second phone conversation with the Smithsonian's maritime curator, Paul Johnston. I told the curator about our search for the mysterious hull section, and he burst out laughing before I got to the punchline. Johnston explained that he had been shown a drawing of the hull when it was found the first time, in '83. The curator knew at a glance that it was at least a hundred years too modern.

I also talked again with the cofferdam archaeologist, Warren Riess. I asked him about the chance of Clifford finding the mother lode. "That's ridiculous," Riess replied. "We were in the mother lode from the beginning."

Peter was talking. "How much treasure do they have?"

"I first heard they had ten thousand *gold and silver* coins. I think the real number is eight thousand three hundred silver coins and *nine* gold coins. As for the value of the treasure, I've seen a silver coin from the *Whydah* selling for $400. Retail. By my calculations, that's less than four million dollars for the lot—not forty million. At auction they might get half that much—unless I write a best-seller, of course."

"What about the gold bars and jewelry?" Peter asked.

"The biggest piece of gold bullion that I saw in the vault is the size of a chocolate-covered marshmallow cookie with a bite taken out. All the gold would fit in one hand. What they call 'jewelry' are mangled bits of African gold beads. The photos make them look as big as golf balls, but they're not much bigger than boogers. The problem with pirates is that they smashed everything into equal shares."

Peter chuckled again. I'd never seen him in such a good mood. He didn't seem to mind that this hour would have sixty minutes in it. Neither did I. So I kept going.

"One gang from the Golden Age sliced a huge diamond into forty-three equal shares. That's hard to beat. But Clifford's gang has tried. They said they found gold dust suspended in the sand like the chocolate in fudge ripple ice cream. But I didn't see much gold dust in the vault. Then one of the archaeologists mentioned that the *Whydah* probably had a stern window made of mica. The divers retrieved a lot of it, he said. The archaeologist didn't know why they bothered, but I have a theory."

"Which is?" said Peter.

"Underwater, flakes of mica shine like gold."

"Fool's gold?" my wife asked.

"Essentially. The divers brought up a piece of red silica and logged it in as a gemstone. They probably thought it was a ruby."

Peter glanced at his watch. "Whoa," he said. "We've gotta stop." He picked up a pencil and paged through his appointment book. "Are we set for next week?"

My wife nodded.

So did I. "I'll be working at Silver Screen Partners."

We all got up. The therapist held out his hand at the door as he always did. "Steve," he said. "I think you ought to drop this book before you get hurt."

I shrugged. "Silver Screen can't complain. They told me to verify everything I heard from Clifford—and that's what I'm doing. The book packager can't complain either. I told the story to my editor there, and she promised to send me a copy of *Liar's Poker*. Lief shut her down, but at least I warned them. I've even confronted Clifford. All he cares is that he can get a job when I'm done, and he can talk his way into anything."

Peter leaned against the door frame and frowned. "Why do you suppose Clifford wants this book?"

"I've got a theory about that, too. Clifford was once a lifeguard. He had a trick where he tied a dead shark to a buoy. Later, when a pretty girl went swimming, he'd called a shark alert and dive into the water with a knife between his teeth."

"So?"

"So Clifford's Catholic. He told the girl afterward. I figure that's my job. I'm supposed to tell the girl she got lured into the sack by a dead shark."

I made it to street level before my wife exploded.

Maria Hallett was more than a character from a folk tale. I was sure of that as I wandered alone down through Central Park toward the duck pond. Edwin Dethlefsen, Ph.D., the aquaprobed archaeologist, did the research for his book *Whidah: Cape Cod's Mystery Treasure Ship.*

Dethlefsen first spent hours chasing Halletts through the *New England Historical and Genealogical Register.* He found Halletts on the Cape by 1656. In 1715, the same year the Spanish treasure fleet wrecked, John Hallett married Mehitable Brown in Eastam, the town next to Orleans where Sam Bellamy is said to have met Maria. John Hallett could have had a younger sister named Maria.

And yet the Harvard-trained archaeologist also found documents that claimed the pirate came from Dorset, England, where he had a wife and children. According to those records, when news of the Spanish wrecks reached Dorset, Bellamy sailed off on his treasure hunt.

Dethlefsen wondered why Bellamy would sail to Eastam on his way to Florida? Eastam was out of Bellamy's way, isolated, and without a harbor. It made no sense.

Then Dethlefsen found a will, dated 1633, in which one Joseph Hallett of Dorset left five shillings to a Marjorie Bellamy. Continuing that line of research, Dethlefsen started bumping into Halletts and Bellamys living close together in England all the way back to 1543. If the two families were connected in England, Bellamy's landfall made perfect sense. Bellamy left his wife and kids in Dorset and sailed to the Cape looking for kin to help him on his treasure hunt. Among them he might have met Maria of the Hallett clan and seduced her with tales of Spanish gold.

The folk tales say Bellamy didn't know that he left Maria pregnant. She bore his child and hid the baby in a barn, where it choked to death on piece of straw. When the body was discovered she was jailed, but the young beauty had such power over her jailers that she could escape at will. Declared a witch and banished to a hut above the cliffs, she wove cloth and waited for the return of her lover.

All of this could have happened. It made perfect sense.

And yet the folk tales didn't stop with the wreck of the *Whydah*. According to Clifford's own primary source—the wonderful book by Elizabeth Reynard called *The Narrow Land: Folk Chronicles of Old Cape Cod*—two survivors from the *Whydah* were captured and taken to Boston. One of them was spotted near Maria's hut. Afterward she never wanted for money, and yet she stayed isolated on the cliffs, watching and waiting:

> That autumn in Eastam, a tall stranger appeared at Higgin's Tavern. His black hair was streaked with white, his dark eyes commanding; but a deep wound scarred his forehead, and his mind was not always clear. Once he called the landlord to see a ship sailing over Eastam Meadows; again he stood quietly, moving his hands as though serving his watch at the wheel. Sometimes he became lost to all sense of reality, and sat in the Great Room, his eyes smoldering, yet in them the look of a bewildered child. He had no lack of money; he lived well, with a highborn manner and his black curly hair. One lock of it, over the scarred temple, had gone winter white.
>
> He died in the summer of 1720 in the apple tree hollow by the burying acre, where he went so often and seemed to be waiting for someone. After he was carried to Higgin's Tavern, a belt of gold was found

on his body; and the men who looked at his face in death said that it was brave and young.

A week later young Thankful Knowles, daughter of Elder John Knowles, took her courage in her capable hands and walked across-dune to get a pattern from Maria. The witch girl was not in her hut, and knowing that she was wont to sit on a ledge by the sea where the *Whydah* lay, Thankful walked to the cliff and peered below. Then she ran, stumbling, breathless, acrossed-dune to the town. For Maria Hallett, dressed in hyacinth blue, with at least a thousand apple blossoms woven over the skirt of her gown, lay stiff on the ledge, her eyes shining, a gash across her white throat and a knife in her hand.

A man leaves his wife to go on a treasure hunt. Buoyed by visions of gold, he seduces a young beauty. When he fails to find the mother lode, he can't go back, and so signs his name in blood to becomes a pirate. He gets his treasure, but he wrecks. He goes mad. He sees ships that aren't there.

Maria's curse.

My thoughts returned to Heidi.

After his knee operation Clifford couldn't ride his mountain bike and had lent it to me. Heidi had a bike of her own, so one sunny afternoon we pedaled to a house perched on the cliffs not far from the Marconi site. The house belonged to one of MEI's investors from Vail, and Clifford thought I could use it through the winter to write. The view from the bedroom was magnificent.

The road to the investor's house skirted the edge of the cliff. In places a shoulder remained on the ocean side, but the previous winter's storms had taken most of it. Fifty yards beyond the house, the road lost one lane. A few yards farther the remaining lane crumbled into space.

The house proved to be locked, and the key was not hidden in any of the places that Heidi remembered. We peered through the windows and then decided to climb down to the beach. No one else was there. We ran a couple miles chasing sand pipers and then jumped into the cold surf wearing our shorts and T-shirts. Hers were white nylon, now transparent. We lay down in the shelter of the cliff.

I reached toward her.

She brushed my hand away. "You're married."

As I looked away I lied to myself that I had touched her only to test her relationship with Clifford.

But of course Clifford was also married when he seduced Heidi. Maybe mine wasn't a fair test. I looked at her again. The sand on her legs was turning white; the nylon, opaque. Her lips were parted. Her eyes closed.

I looked away. "What's the difference between Bellamy and Barry?" I asked.

Heidi propped herself up on her elbows and stared out to sea. "Barry would have made it back," she said.

Then I thought: no, making it back was not the difference. Sam Bellamy must have survived the wreck. The pirate went mad, but he came back.

Heidi got up and walked to the water's edge. I watched her go imagining her as Maria Hallett, scanning the horizon for sails.

She turned and beckoned, and I realized then that I was watching for Jennifer as she emerged from the waves at the Bahamas Diamond Triathlon of the Stars. I started thinking how I seduced her with tales of Olympic gold in Los Angeles. Then the Mercedes. The penthouse. The deals. The deals. The deals.

Heidi had found something in the sand. She bent over and came up with a shell, smiling like the girl on the Newport poster.

In my own selfish ways I had tried to make my wife happy, but I was also coming to understand that part of the problem was beyond me. When Jennifer was in high school, her father ran off with a pretty young blonde—and in the process had somehow knocked Jennifer through a glass door, cutting her wrist. Her mother then forced Jennifer to write letters begging him to come home.

Those letters...

Writing them would have destroyed me. After the letters and a summer nightmare hitchhiking on Martha's Vineyard, it was a wonder my wife could speak to men at all.

My wife didn't really trust me. And why should she?

And so, watching Heidi on the beach, I came up with a new plan.

The only dream I ever heard Jennifer's father mention was to someday moor his fishing boat on a buoy off his in-laws' house on Contentment Island. I now figured that all it would take to start over again was for him to say, "I was an asshole. Forgive me. *Take my boat.*" He wouldn't have to say anything if he just tossed her the keys.

In the meantime, however, I looked at Heidi coming toward me, smiling, and I felt empty. Later, riding back on Tonsett Road, I spotted Clifford's Saab coming toward us and felt like a cockroach.

Clifford pulled over, got out, and inspected us. He smiled at me—as cruel a smile as I have ever seen.

I marveled at the smile.

And I shivered.

When I returned to Manhattan, I called Chip McGrath at *The New Yorker* to hear his response to my proposal for a profile of Clifford. I was now counting on it. Desperate for it. But McGrath passed. He mentioned seeing my name in the announcement of *The Pirate Prince* in *Publishers Weekly*. He wished me luck.

My throat constricted. I couldn't talk. I couldn't breathe.

Once years ago my raft flipped in the Colorado River and dumped me into a hole formed by water pouring over a boulder—a keeper. Buoyed by my lifejacket against the current, I could see sunlight through the water but couldn't reach it. The only thing to do was turn upside-down and go for the bottom.

What amazed me was the size of the fish under the rock.

Wall Street on Parade

Tom Bernstein slides open a closet door. Inside,
the face of Mickey Mouse, holding Silver Screen
III logos, grins from a dozen red satin jackets.
"Aren't these great?" Bernstein asks. Then he plucks
a graduation cap with Mickey Mouse ears from a
box and proudly announces that caps like this one
are for Hutton brokers who sell the partnerships
created by his company...

The American Lawyer, April 1988

The file was labeled Lief Contract, and I couldn't take my
eyes off it. I pulled other files first, such as History and Maritime Explorer, and felt like a kid at a newsstand gathering
Smithsonian and *Time* before whimsically snagging a *Playboy*. Finally my stack of files was thick enough that I felt
comfortable slipping the Lief Contract into the middle. I hur-
ried back to my desk, displayed the other files, and I spun

around in my chair to read the Wall Streeters' contract with the book packager.

That morning was already far gone on a bad start. I had mangled my gray suit while dragging my Macintosh through the subway. Then I threw out my back in the turnstile. At Silver Screen Partners I just wanted to hide—and expected to be shown to one of the small cubicles tucked away in the back. Instead, to my astonishment, I got a power office with a view up Broadway. Shown the supply room, the coffee machine, the washroom, the copiers and the files, I was told I could stay as late as I wanted and for as long. "Make yourself at home!" So I tried. But everyone else was so nice and so well put together that I felt like a virus. Then I sat down in my ergonomically designed chair at my Danish modern desk and discovered that only a well-put-together person could work in such a space. There was a door to shut, but it and the surrounding wall were made of glass. Scratching, exploring my nostrils, picking my nails and other necessities of my dubious trade would be impossible.

Nevertheless, I felt flattered until I opened the Lief file. This wasn't *Playboy*. It was *Hustler.*

Clifford and Lief's original contract had split the movie rights equally. My share was 10% of Lief's share, so I got 5%—maybe dinner at the Russian Tea Room. But that contract became worthless when Bernstein and Betts stepped in—and so they had worked Lief over. It was such a good job that the bruises didn't show—and Lief hadn't let on—but he must have been in some pain. Lief's share of the movie rights had been slashed to 15%. My share was cab fare.

Nobody was playing straight.

For about three weeks, during November 1989, I went on a treasure hunt at Silver Screen Partners, working through the *Whydah* files from A to Z. I read thousands of pages of memos, notes, clippings, and reports. There were proposals for children's books, catalogues for dive equipment, and insurance records from the infamous flagship *Maritime Exploder*. A screenplay treatment had been written about the *Whydah*. The Harvard Business School had done a case study. My hardest job was to find the treasure among the dud ordnance and shrapnel—a job that might have been overwhelming, except for the plan. The Media Plan. It was written shortly after the cannons were found—during a four-month-long press blackout that MEI imposed. The plan was filed under "Konkapot," the marketing company formed by Clifford, Betts, and the Bernsteins.

"Whidah"
Business and Media Plan

October 5, 1984

Robert L. Bernstein
Tom A. Bernstein
Roland W. Betts

Having concluded this preliminary phase and having visited the *Vast Explorer II*, we are confident that Maritime Explorations has found the "Whidah." We are now prepared to take an active role in the management of the venture.

It is imperative that we go forward with the understanding that our Corporation will have control of all major decisions, marketing and exploitation of the "Whidah" project....

The reason for this tight control is that our effective use of the media is directly connected to our overall business objectives. The media we will cooperate with in the months ahead will be carefully selected to provide us with print and television coverage that will, in words and pictures, tell the story that we want to tell. Our view is that carefully controlled, publicized, managed, financed, marketed and exploited, the Whidah project can generate enormous long-term benefits for all those involved. Our task is to make that happen....

It is important for the press to report that the excavation is being conducted by trained archaeologists and other experts who are interested in treating the find as part of the cultural heritage of our country, rather than as a way to make a quick buck....

Further on, the two Bernsteins and Betts described their progress:

We have already finalized arrangements with Eric Copage at Life Magazine for Life to do a major photo essay on the "Whidah." Although Life only has a circulation of 1.6 million, the photo essay will be of great value as a "selling document" in attracting financing and exploiting rights to the project.

In addition, Robert Bernstein had discussions with Walter Anderson, the editor of Parade Magazine (circulation 24 million and readership of 51 million), about doing a series of articles on the Whidah. The writer Anderson has in mind is David White (Theodore White's son) who is an expert on marine archaeology and is a seasoned diver. Later in the fall, we may also want to arrange for a feature story in The New York Times.

During the press blackout, while the powerful New Yorkers were orchestrating the best possible places to release the pirate story to the world, Barry Clifford was figuring out what the story might say. By then MEI had brought ashore the first cannon, which was covered in barnacles and had a .50 caliber machine-gun shell concreted to it. In his log November 5,

1984, Clifford made some notes for a member of the state board:

> 1. Thousands of <extremely rare> coins. (many are extremely rare).
> 2. pirate weapons ect. (perfect condition)
> 3. high concentration in one 100 TP [100 square-foot test pit]
> 4. has never been sal. [salvaged]

I then dug around in my pile of papers to see how the marketing effort paid off in *Parade*:

The Man Who Found a 400 Million Dollar Pirate's Treasure

by David White:

Diving off the Massachusetts town of Wellfleet, a modern day adventurer named Barry Clifford has uncovered what is believed to be the wreck of the W*hidah,* a pirate ship that sank within sight of the beach and with it what promises to be the largest sunken treasure ever retrieved off the continental United States. Already a spectacular fortune in coins, ingots, jewelry, weapons and artifacts has been brought up; And if, as experts are rapidly concluding, the find is in fact the Whidah, the flagship of the notorious 18th Century buccaneer — *a treasure worth at least $400 million is on board.*

More important though, is the historical scope of the find...

By the time *Parade* published the article, Robert Bernstein had dropped out of Konkapot Partners and had given his shares in the company to his children. But the Wall Streeters continued to use the connections made by the Random House chairman, as the Media Plan continued:

It may also be worthwhile to have "60 Minutes" or one of the news magazines like 20/20 do a shorter piece on the project. Programs like this are extremely helpful in focusing national media attention and stimulating book, film and merchandising interest. Robert Bernstein knows the key news executives at the networks and will handle this aspect of the project....

About two and a half weeks after the *Parade* article was published, Walter Cronkite came to Silver Screen's offices to meet with Tom Bernstein, Betts, and Clifford. On February 28, 1985 the Wall Streeters wrote to Cronkite:

This memorandum is to formally propose the structure for the Whidah production company that we discussed at our office on February 14th.

The structure we have in mind is as follows. Walter Cronkite, Barry Clifford and Konkapot Partners will form a production company to produce a two hour CBS television movie with documentary "bookends"—that is, an introduction and post script...

This company will be owned 15% by Barry Clifford, 42.5% by Walter Cronkite and 42.5% by Konkapot Partners. Clifford will sell his rights in the project to CBS and the compensation he receives for the rights will be paid directly to him... Similarly, all payment to Walter Cronkite for his service as "talent"...will be paid directly to Cronkite....

On June 13, Tom Bernstein followed up with another memo to Cronkite:

> I dug out of our file some of the swashbuckler accounts of Barry Clifford. It's hard to tell what is true and what is embellished story telling.
>
> In any event Barry and his lawyer have agreed that we will have final editorial approval on the documentary. I will confirm this in writing.

The proposed movie bounced around New York and Los Angeles for a year or two before it died. However, on October 22, 1986, the *Cape Cod Times* photographed Cronkite in the same motorboat with Clifford, doing an interview for *Cronkite at Large*.

And so it had all happened according to The Media Plan. And the plan wasn't finished:

> Among the book possibilities is the story of Barry Clifford and the "Whidah" excavation. Such a book would include the tale of Barry Clifford (and his band of modern day "pirates") and the historical tale of Black Sam Bellamy, Maria Hallett and the pirates of yesteryear. The first step, of course, is to find an author to work with Barry....

I looked around my power office at Silver Screen wondering if the *Parade* writer had been given one as well—and wondering what would happen to me if I wrote something different from what the Media Plan called for.

When Betts and the Bernsteins wrote the Media Plan, one thing they would *not* do for the *Whydah* project was raise money. Silver Screen was still a fledgling firm financing flops, and Betts wasn't about to risk his credibility on a pirate ship. A year later, however, Betts would be making a fortune with Disney. About the same time, in September, 1985, Betts received a memo from a vice president of the E. F. Hutton Liaison Service Inc:

Opportunity Financing:
An Introduction and a Request

In response to what we believe is a lucrative but unmet investor need, we at E.F. Hutton have geared up to provide a new service, which with your assistance, should be a success to you, the investor and E.F. Hutton....

We are convinced that there has developed a void at the upper echelon where the heretofore sophisticated, big ticket investor is now being inadequately served...

Our study indicates that there is significant unsatisfied demand for well-structured, well priced investments for placement to an individual alone, or in a partnership structure, to a small group of these large investors. In addition, we are aware of your ability to provide quality investments which for reasons of size timing or load would not be suitable for marketing as a standard public offering or private placement...

It is important that the investments you provide for this market not detract from or reduce the supply available to our established retail client base. In fact we are looking specifically for investments with the same economic strength but perhaps because of their size, timing, load or extraordinary characteristics would not be an easy fit with your traditional line or ours...

Betts filed the letter under "Whydah General Concept." Meanwhile, Clifford hit his grand slam, the front pager in *The New York Times,* November 1, 1985:

Bell Confirms That Salvors Found
Pirate Ship of Legend

...Mr. Clifford appears to have established irrefutably the provenance of thousands of coins and

> hundreds of pounds of other artifacts as well as the
> fate of the Whydah....
> The treasure may run into the hundreds of
> millions of dollars....
> ...So far seven cannon, nine sets of navigation
> equipment, and jewelry, gold and other booty has
> been raised, all from two 8-by-8-foot pits. The
> salvage area may eventually cover 100,000 square
> feet."

Bernstein and Betts now felt confident in offering clients a piece of the pirate ship—especially since Cronkite and Disney were involved. To do so, however, they first had to beat the competition.

Clifford had been courting other sources of funding—especially a financier named Jesse Greenfield. The day the bell was to be hauled up from the bottom, Greenfield would have been aboard the *Vast Explorer* had not Clifford gone ballistic in his inflatable and flipped them backward into Nauset Inlet. Undaunted by the dunking—or perhaps inspired by it—Greenfield arranged a $3.5 million offering for the spring of 1986. Clifford seemed committed to the deal, but changed his mind when E.F. Hutton expressed interest in a larger offering.

Clifford stalled Greenfield, and then the tax laws changed, forcing the financier to alter his terms. Once the structure was changed, however, Greenfield was informed that he had broken the deal and that Clifford was free to court other investors. One of the lawyers wrote notes "to the file" from his final conversation with Greenfield: "I wish you well, good luck," said Greenfield. "I just don't want anything more to do with you." According to the lawyer, Greenfield "simply could not do business on this basis, was angry at the time he had wasted with us, and was generally disgusted and disillusioned."

Thus in June 1986, the path was cleared for E.F. Hutton.

Like the original *Whydah* pirates, The Wall Streeters' first job was to divide the loot. On Halloween 1986, their new company, Whydah Management, developed its *Final Summary of Whydah Cash Flow Scenario.* In order for Whydah Management to "break even" on a five-million-dollar investment—taking into account the time value of money and their split with MEI—the treasure auction would have to gross $28.9 million. If the state successfully defended its claim to 25% of the treasure, the auction total would have to bring in much more—about $41 million. Then, because of rising fees, Hutton's offering was increased to six million dollars. Presumably, the break-even point rose at well.

E.F. Hutton's investors were brought in to find a mother lode to sell at auction. The Wall Streeters were clear on that. After all, Bernstein and Betts, through Konkapot and the Media Plan, already controlled the *Whydah* story—and hadn't made money with it. The value of the pirate story was considered significant only because it might raise the auction price of the treasure.

Meanwhile, Clifford and the Media Plan continued to play their parts.

On August 25, 1986, the Associated Press reported:

> *Whydah salvor thinks mother lode still untapped*
>
> Survivors of the *Whydah* testified in the Boston trial the ship contained 30,000 pounds of silver, 10,000 pounds of gold, 20 tons of ivory and jewels from the East Indies. Clifford said estimates of the total value of the treasure range up to $400 million...

In Clifford's own account, published in the November 1986 issue of *Arts & Antiques,* he wrote:

> During the summer of 1984, as many as 3,000
> eighteenth century Spanish coins came out a single
> eight-inch-by-eight-inch test pit.

Clifford did not explain how so many coins might fit into a hole the size of shoebox. He also wrote:

> Thus far only 120 feet of a 100,000 square foot
> scatter pattern has been uncovered, and it will
> probably take us five more years to complete our
> salvage operation.

What a marvelous time! Wall Street was booming. Hutton's offering was growing. The treasure was expanding. Clifford's pits were shrinking. Walter Cronkite was reporting. And no one was paying attention to what MEI's archaeologists were publishing.

By the end of the 1986 dive season, both the perimeter and core of the wreck site had been established from the 15 state-authorized test pits. In the Annual Report, field archaeologist Rob Reedy estimated the total site to include about 24,000 to 27,000 square feet. From Reedy's diagrams, one can see that Clifford's discovery pit in 1984 had been in about the center of the "impact area." Not surprisingly, the magnetometer had led Clifford to the highest concentration of artifacts, the spot where the *Whydah* had turned upside down. From that impact area, the concentration of artifacts diminished rapidly toward the edge of the site, where the test pits were essentially free of artifacts. In other words, Clifford hit the mother lode on his very first pit.

The prospectus for Hutton's offering is a blue-gray bound volume the size of a school workbook and about half an inch thick. The cover has a drawing of a ship under full sail flying a black flag with a skull and crossbones. When Tom Bernstein presented me with the prospectus, he said it contained the whole story of the *Whydah*. The boilerplate reads:

Further on, the investor was warned:

...estimates attributed to Maritime Explorations or its agents in the media, as to the quantity and value of the Recovered Objects already excavated or potentially salvageable may be highly speculative and exaggerated. The General Partner specifically disclaims all such representations and estimates.

Curious, I checked the index for Konkapot, and found it where it should have been, under "Conflicts of Interest." The explanation, however, was not what I expected:

...Konkapot will manage and control the marketing of all rights arising from Maritime Explorations excavation of sunken ships *other than the Whydah*. Essentially the Konkapot Agreement grants Konkapot the same rights with regard to Exploitation of Maritime Explorations *non-Whydah* activities as the Joint Venture has with respect to the *Whydah* Ancillary Rights.

In other words, the prospectus mentioned only the possibility of future conflicts with other MEI projects—such as the *Hussar* in the East River. The Wall Streeters chose not to explain the conflicts of the past, when their Media Plan instigated the media hoopla they now expected investors to ignore.

Not surprisingly, given the nature of the investment, the Wall Streeters protected themselves with a list of risk factors: 26 factors covering over 13 pages. The list started with the basics: 1. *The Ship Might not be the Whydah,* and 2. *The Quantity of Artifacts Cannot be Ascertained.* Gradually the list worked toward 25. *Risk of Total Loss,* and presumably worse, 26. *Risks Relating to Federal Income Tax Considerations.*

Most amusing, however, was risk 8:

> *The Reliance on Certain Personnel.* If the services of Mssrs. Clifford and/or McClung become unavailable for any reason, however, the excavation and salvage of the permit area could be jeopardized and there could be material adverse effect upon future operation.

But the prospectus left out a possible corollary, 8-B:

> If the services of Mr. Clifford becomes *available* for any reason, the excavation and salvage of the permit area could also be jeopardized...

A few pages later, in his biography, Clifford illustrated the importance of this corollary:

> In 1976, Mr. Clifford discovered the *Benedict Arnold* off Plymouth, Massachusetts; the *Benedict Arnold* was a 1778 American Revolutionary War Privateer which was the first such shipwreck ever located in this country...

Clifford illustrated the corollary again in his description of the excavation:

> As part of this first phase Maritime Explorations excavated fifteen experimental test pits to obtain detailed data necessary to design its overall salvage program...
>
> As a result of the test pits excavated to date Maritime believes that it has identified the approximate location and perimeter of the wreck site and the core excavation area where it believes that many of the ship's artifacts are located.
>
> If it determines that a sufficient number of Units have been sold to allow substantial implementation of the Full Plan, Maritime Explorations intends to purchase a second, larger salvage boat. In 1988 and 1989, Maritime intends to excavate the remainder of the core area.

Clifford didn't mention Frank Wells' wild dives into Disneyland—or the mats of mung that archaeologists would stumble upon for years to come. When Hutton's offering was sold, how much of the core area actually remained unexplored?

While an offering is in process, those associated with the company selling the stock typically refrain from making public statements to insure that investors rely only on information printed in their prospectus. According to an SEC spokesman, there is no inherent conflict between the First Amendment and securities laws. On the other hand, "The quiet period is a gray area where even lawyers fear to tread."

Because ignoring the quiet period can expose a company to enormous lawsuits, E.F. Hutton couldn't be too cautious. At least a couple of incidents were considered. For example, the Harvard Business School was using MEI as a case study in entrepreneurial financing and asked one of MEI's lawyers to give a lecture. Would that speech violate the quiet period?

The answer was probably yes, but the lawyer gave the speech anyway because it was a small class and at Harvard.

Whydah Management also worried about a speech Clifford was scheduled to give to the American Dental Association on May 17. The memo, dated April 28, read "While we hope to close [the offering] by that date, I just wanted to make sure you were aware that this speaking engagement would be in violation of the quiet period."

Also in the file was a memo, dated January 28, from Tom Bernstein to the president of Columbia Pictures. Bernstein wrote, "We are about to raise $6 million through Hutton," and "Walter Cronkite has completed a documentary segment to air this spring."

Curious, I got a copy of the documentary and watched it through—from Cronkite's description of "tons of gold, silver, indigo and ivory" to his closing statement:

> So the question remains: How much *Whydah* treasure is buried in that Atlantic sand? And what will it be worth when it is put on the auction block?
>
> A large Wall Street firm is raising six million dollars to finance the continuing venture. Some of that offering has been snapped up by the firm's employees. It is not something Wall Streeters say they would offer to people planning their retirement. On the other hand, the auction house Sotheby's is said to be interested in the first items that are put up for sale.

Hutton's offering opened March 5.

Cronkite's CBS News special aired March 30.

Hutton's offering closed May 28.

The most trusted man in America broadcast his prime-time special smack in the middle of E.F. Hutton's stock offering.

This would have been a good time to pack up my Macintosh

and my photocopies, walk a few blocks, and throw it all into the East River. Otherwise, I might discover that America's most trusted public figure had violated SEC regulations. And that concept could prove profoundly destabilizing. If Cronkite turned out to be a crook, then, for example, Richard Nixon might turn out to be a hero.

Nah.

This story couldn't be true. I just wasn't looking at it right.

Besides, my treasure hunt was far from finished. In Silver Screen's files was another clue. The unsigned cover letter read:

> The document is not only important from an historical standpoint, but is also most significant in determining the contemporary issue as to the final fate of Captain Samuel Bellamy and his pirate treasure. The document speaks for itself.

Stapled to it was a photocopy of a handwritten deposition dated May 12, 1717—as well as a typescript. Portions of the typescript were highlighted in yellow marker.

> There are 19 of the pirates and they told us they were the only men that escaped that belonged to the ship that run aground on shore at Cape Cod, and they made their escape in the longboat.

> They kept us prisoner about twelve hours, in which time they took what goods that was on board their sloop, which was several chests, trunks and bale goods, and brought them aboard our sloop.

> And (the pirates) said that they had taken three sloops and three schooners that belonged to Marblehead and had set them at liberty again to go about their business and did them no damage.

The document, known as the Newman Deposition, arrived at the *Cape Cod Times* without a signature or return address. The three highlighted statements were quoted in a front-page article that began:

> Nineteen pirates from the ship *Whydah*—if not black bearded Capt. Samuel Bellamy—may have survived when the galley smashed to pieces off Marconi Beach in 1717.

The *Times* article was dated January 16, 1987—almost two months before Hutton's stock offering.

Just what was in those chests and trunks? What about those bale goods? Why was there no mention of nineteen possible survivors in Hutton's prospectus?

Yo Ho Ho! 19 Men and a Dead Man's Chests

I first suspected "claim jumper" Matt Costa of sending the Newman Deposition to the newspapers, and so I drove to Provincetown and walked unannounced into his headquarters, a fish market. It was on a side street after dark: closing time. The lights were dim and the place writhed with lobsters. Huge lobsters. Back-lit, their shadows scuttled on the floor and walls, a ghastly vision made more so by the stench of fresh disinfectant. And then came Costa. He approached slowly from the rear, swaying back and forth rhythmically with what looked like a spear. But like a shadow Costa got smaller as he got nearer until he looked like a coxswain wearing a black eye patch.

Costa put down the mop. "We're closed."

No, Costa didn't have a deposition about 19 pirates in a longboat. He hadn't threatened Clifford with a pistol either.

Costa owned a fish market and, on the side, collected stuff salvaged by fishermen. He filed for a salvage permit on the *White Squall* (just north of MEI) mainly to keep Clifford from claiming the entire coastline. There had been plenty of flotsam and jetsam for everybody until Clifford came along.

Hoping to cheer Costa up, I bought a couple lobsters and left.

So much for that.

Opposite Costa's permit area, on Clifford's southern flank, the salvage permit was owned by the Old Blue Fishing Company, led by one William Crockett. Clifford dismissed Crockett as a nice guy who never went to college and got the *Whydah* story all wrong. I phoned Crockett at his home in Chatham. After some hesitation he invited me over.

The address proved to be only a few blocks from the stretch of pricey tourist shops like the Spyglass, but Crockett's house was cramped and old, a real seafarer's home. Crockett looked as if he had stepped out of a painting by Winslow Homer. Stocky, with a grizzled mustache and a face gnarled by countless storms, Crockett wore nothing over his closed eye socket.

I held out my hand. He took it grudgingly, and I understood then what a horny palm was. His body blocked the door.

"Every time I hear Clifford's name I end up with lawyer bills," he said. "I don't need that anymore. Never did. If that's where talking to you is going to end up, you should leave right now." His voice while gruff was not flat.

I mumbled something about planning to avoid lawyers.

"So what do you want to talk about?"

"Finding the *Whydah.*" I shrugged. "I want to figure out how Clifford really did it—*if* he really did it."

"Give me a for instance."

"Okay. Cyprian Southack's treasure map. I want to know

how Clifford found it. He said something about a library at Harvard, but I don't know."

Crockett's response was a look of incredulous detachment as if facing a complete and pitiable idiot.

"Where you from?" he asked.

"New York City."

"You eat at the diners round here?"

"Yeah. Sure."

"Well then, you've probably spilled your coffee on Southack's map. It's printed on the menus."

"Oh." I said finally. "No shit."

Crockett's laugh was not unfriendly. "You might as well come in. You want some coffee?"

I don't remember much about the interior of the house except that the rooms were small and full of stuff: papers and photos and strange objects. So far as I could tell he lived alone. "Nice photograph," I said, noticing a black and white of the Great Wall of China. It *was* a good photograph. "Who took it?"

"It's mine."

I scanned another photo. "Where are these mountains?

"Tibet."

"You've got a good eye."

As soon as I said it, I felt like an ass. But the comment didn't faze Crockett. He explained that he had lost his eye to a fishhook. Fishing was his job—as was painting houses. Such work allowed him the time and money to travel and take photographs. He had been all over the world.

We left the living room and went down a hall to the kitchen, a place probably equipped in the forties and not changed since. Crockett put water on the stove and rinsed two dirty cups from the sink. We sat on vinyl chairs at the kitchen table, and he pushed some cooking pots out of the way for elbow room. He seemed to have forgotten about lawyers. I asked how he got involved with the *Whydah*.

"In Chatham Harbor I saw a black PT-boat with 'Marine Research' painted along the side in big red letters," he replied. "The crew kept to themselves, but I recognized the mailboxes and guessed what they were up to. The captain, Kirk Purvis, had just come down from New Hampshire where he was looking for a wreck from Admiral Drake's fleet. Kirk's crew was ready to walk, and so I signed on. It wasn't anything like the bullshit today. The operation was quiet and small. Discreet. If Kirk and I had hit it, no one would ever have known. We would have split the treasure fifty-fifty."

"When was that?"

"Twenty years ago. Fall of seventy-one."

Crockett sighed and got up to tend the coffee. "We found every wreck out there—the *Castagna, White Squall,* a bunch of fishing boats—everything but the *Whydah*. Kirk quit at the end of the fall, but I had the bug. I went to the state archives and read all of the obvious material, such as Southack's notes and the transcripts of the pirate trials. I figured the real stuff was in England."

"You go there?"

"Four times. In seventy-four, seventy-eight, eighty-one, and the last time in eighty-four. I copied hundreds of documents."

Crockett's tale went on. His research taught him the horrors of the slave trade, the corrupt politics in Jamaica in 1717, and the possibility that the captain of the *Whydah*, Lawrence Prince, had been in cahoots with Sam Bellamy. From Crockett I learned that a community of people around the Cape had searched for pieces of the *Whydah* story, men and women who traded documents like baseball cards. When Clifford arrived, he took their documents or he branded them as claim jumpers and battered them with lawsuits.

Crockett shrugged. "Clifford took all the fun out of it."

"As soon as somebody found the wreck, it was over," Crockett continued. But it wasn't. Not quite. Crockett left the kitchen, and I followed him into the living room where he opened a closet crammed with junk. Near the top was a shelf stacked with papers. He grabbed the stack and lay the papers on the floor. On top was the Newman Deposition.

"The newspapers were looking for stories," Crockett said with a grin.

I got down on my knees next to Crockett to inspect the document. It looked to me a deal-breaker. But it wasn't that simple. Ken Kinkor, MEI's piratologist, claimed the Deposition was wrong. Kinkor said that 18 pirates from Bellamy's gang were aboard Bellamy's final prize, a sloop from Viginia that was captured just before the fatal storm broke. The sloop was probably damaged in the storm, and the 18 might have taken to their longboat. The pirates might have claimed they "belonged" to the *Whydah* because it was the flagship. They might have called themselves the "only" survivors, since they probably didn't know that others had escaped the storm.

I poked at the Deposition. "Ken Kinkor thinks this is nonsense."

"Yeah?" said Crockett. "And where does his paycheck come from? Without that stock offering, Kinkor would have been pounding the pavement."

True enough, I figured. "Could nineteen men have escaped the wreck?"

"Sure," Crockett said. "At their trial the pirates mentioned lightning. That meant the storm was a southeaster—not so violent as a northeaster. The pirates knew they weren't going to sail free, and so they turned straight for the beach. Fifteen minutes elapsed between the time the ship hit the bar and when it lost its mainmast and capsized—plenty of time to launch a longboat. Cotton Mather claimed there was fighting aboard the *Whydah* before she broke up, which would make sense if there were one hundred and eighty men aboard and only one longboat."

Crockett went on about something else, but I was distracted. E.F. Hutton's prospectus claimed that eight *Whydah* survivors were taken to Boston to stand trial. That wasn't accurate. Only two of the surviving pirates—a Cape Cod Indian and a carpenter—were aboard the *Whydah* that night. Another seven pirates were aboard one of Bellamy's prizes, the *Mary Anne*, a cargo vessel filled with wine. The *Mary Anne* ran aground in the storm, and the pirates were captured.

Hutton's error had seemed insignificant—until now.

The Cape Indian disappeared from the record and is presumed to have died in jail. The carpenter was acquitted. In other words, the only man to stand trial who knew what happened aboard the *Whydah* that night went free—and disappeared into history. If 19 pirates sailed off with the treasure—the chests, trunks and bale goods—the carpenter would have no incentive to tell anyone. So long as he kept his mouth shut, he might still collect his share.

Just what the folk tales said.

Crockett was chuckling. "How much treasure do you suppose those Wall Streeters have? Come on, you've seen it." He slapped my thigh. "How much? A million dollars worth? Less? What do you think?"

"I think they've lost their marbles."

Crockett winked. He was also laughing at me. For a moment I joined him, and it felt good.

At Christmas, Darien's Contentment Island was awash in presents, but as tense as always. I got drunk and tried to convince my father-in-law to let Jennifer use his boat. I suggested as gently as I could that perhaps his daughter didn't really believe he loved her, and maybe a boat ride would help.

[Warning: Professional journalist: Don't try this at home.]

Afterward, Jennifer and I took off on a vacation. She was desperate for someplace warm, and I chose Florida. I told her we'd fly to Palm Beach and drive to the Keys. Then maybe drive back up the gulf coast. It would be a lot of driving for just one week, but we'd have fun. I casually interjected that Aspen's former police chief Rob McClung was in West Palm, Judge John Levin was in Key West, and MEI's first archaeologist, Ted Dethlefsen, was in Tampa. My wife was less than ecstatic, but at least she'd be warm.

I figured the key to the *Whydah* puzzle was the police chief.

Once while McClung was diving, Clifford fiddled with the pressure gauges on deck and shut off the air. McClung sucked his hose dry and had to swim to the surface, unclamp his dive helmet, and hold the neck of his dry suit above the waves to keep from drowning. Later, while diving on the *Hussar*, McClung and another diver got their umbilicals snagged on the bottom of the East River. Clifford, who was monitoring them from above, had an appointment on shore and began yelling at the divers to hurry. When McClung told Clifford to shut up so the divers could hear each other, Clifford kicked the monitor station, jumped into a Whaler and motored ashore—leaving his best friend snagged on the river bottom.

A pattern perhaps? But why?

A new theory:

Clifford lied to me that his real father was a pilot in the Army Air Corps who was shot down and killed. McClung's father, a pilot with the Flying Tigers, was shot down and wounded. Clifford claimed to have been a football star; at Western State, however, he was dropped to third or fourth string before he got thrown off the team. McClung played first string. McClung was Florida's diving champion in high school and spent his spare time spearfishing and wreck diving. McClung taught Clifford to scuba dive. McClung found the cannons. McClung found the bell.

McClung would know exactly how the wreck was located and how many pits were dug. That might explain why Clifford didn't want me talking to him. Clifford might not want the chief talking to anybody.

But at the last moment before Jennifer and I flew to Florida, McClung called to cancel our meeting. I pinned my hopes on Judge Levin. Over the phone the former judge hadn't been cooperative. He said he might talk to *The New York Times*, but that might mean calling a grand jury. He did offer one piece of advice:

"Follow the money."

The Size of the Flies

"When a veteran treasure hunter gets *serious* about launching a search, he goes looking for bikinis," said John Levin, the former Colorado judge and the original financial officer of MEI. Levin was now putting away a sheaf of navigation charts and sub-bottom profiles, computer-drawn diagrams that might lead him and some lucky investors to Blackbeard's treasure. Levin wanted me to see the treasure charts. He just didn't want me to look at them.

"This bar is perfect," Levin continued, nodding over the deck railing toward the hotel swimming pool where a score of young women in tanning-wear had arranged themselves like tropical flowers. "You can write an equation for it." He took a gold pen from his leather aviator's jacket and applied himself to a cocktail napkin. "It's simple," he said. "The flow of investment money rises inversely with the amount of material used in a bathing suit. The smaller the suits, the more money is around. This town was built by wreckers. The sun is hot, the drinks are strong, and the bikinis are as small as the law allows. It makes men feel like kids again. Here in Key West, treasure deals are put together every day."

I reached for the napkin—now an abstract of dollar signs and bikini lines—but Levin glared and crumpled it up. I sat back in my chair and drained my *piña colada*.

Maybe it was the sun or the rum or maybe it was Levin. I was exhausted. The judge was looking elsewhere so I inspected him: shoulder-length black hair, aviator's jacket, white silk scarf, mirrored shades. After his divorce the judge had stepped down from the bench with a mental disability pension. Still, if you get a pension for being mentally disabled, how disabled can you be?

This man had solved *Catch-22*.

Levin had told me that he started his career in the late sixties as a New York assistant DA, and that he got involved with the Serpico police corruption trials. Death threats, among other things, soured him on the Big Apple, and so he moved to Crested Butte, Colorado, a Wild West town over the pass from Aspen. He became a municipal judge.

In court Levin met a local marshal, Rob McClung, who had written a ticket for someone smoking a joint outside the Grubstake Saloon. In the early seventies, writing a ticket for drug possession was a novel and lenient procedure, and the judge, who had smoked dope himself, was intrigued. The marshal and the judge took heat from the press and from other police departments for writing and accepting the ticket. They became friends.

Oddly enough, McClung hated drugs. His older brother Randy got into acid while with the Green Berets in the 101st Airborne. After his discharge, Randy started smuggling. While sailing back from the Bahamas, Randy's girlfriend disappeared overboard. No one knows how, but everyone aboard claimed she must have fallen. Because of the drug connection, however, the FBI investigated a possible homicide. Randy had planned to marry the girl, and he mentioned his distress over the investigation in his suicide note.

When McClung moved to Aspen to be chief of police, Levin became an adviser to the department and often rode along on drug raids. The judge enjoyed the adventure so much that McClung lent him a .357 magnum pistol. In return, Levin helped smooth things when the chief's efforts proved over-enthusiastic. Levin proved particularly helpful when the chief led an assault team against what was supposed to be a narcotics distribution center and a cache of weapons. When the suspect opened the door to his condo, he was hoisted by his bathrobe and conveyed overhead along a line of officers and dumped head-first into the snow. The condo was ransacked, and no drugs or guns were found. The judge soothed the owner while the officers restored everything as best they could and vacuumed the floors.

Then the long-lost owner of a stolen .357 magnum came to Aspen's Police Department to pick up his gun. The pistol was not in the property locker. Instead, it turned up in the chief's desk. About the same time, McClung asked Levin to return the .357 magnum. Although McClung claimed otherwise, almost everyone assumed that it was the same .357. When the story was picked up by the press, the chief was crucified. He resigned from the force and joined the treasure hunt—where the judge was now Clifford's financial officer.

Levin said he decided to leave MEI when he came into Clifford's room late one night and found him huddled over the charts, stark naked, measuring the body of a dead fly on the chart table to calculate where to dig the next day with the

Vast Explorer. Levin said he would have quit immediately but he had already raised tens of thousands of dollars from his friends in Colorado. He figured he might be liable.

A new tropical flower promenaded by the pool taking my eyes with her. She was wrapped in something shiny. She stopped, scanned the scene until all eyes were upon her, and shed the wrap. The remaining strings, as thin as the law allowed, weren't structural.

"Ain't nature wonderful," I mumbled at Levin.

He shook his head. "Don't count on it."

He was right: her breasts stayed up as she lay down. She applied oil topside, rolled over prone, and pulled the strings across her back, untying the bow. She raised herself on her elbows to readjust and then lay back down. There was no oil on her back. The bottle lay beside her.

Levin was saying something, but I wasn't paying attention.

It probably wouldn't matter.

It just had to.

I scribbled in the air toward the waitress, and turned to the judge. "I've got to meet my wife." I gathered up my notebook. "By the way, what do you think happened to the treasure of the *Whydah*?"

The judge drained his glass, set it down, and laughed. "The longboat carried 19 guys. Bellamy knew they were going to wreck and said, 'Bring me gold and jewels.' The bale goods were silk. If they didn't have all the gold and jewels in the longboat, they wouldn't have taken the silk."

The day after my conversation with Levin in Key West, my wife and I drove north to Tampa for what I swore would be the last interview of my research. I left her at the hotel and drove to a neighborhood of cracked sidewalks strewn with torn garbage bags. The address proved to be a gray clapboard that might once have been a fine fixer-upper. I climbed the steps onto a sagging wood porch, knocked, and waited. Eventually, the door opened a crack, then further, and I met a grandfatherly man with a flowing white beard. He was not particularly old, but he was broken—alone and lonely. His wife had left him, or vice versa. His possessions, mostly books and video equipment, were scattered about as if he had just moved in.

It was Edwin Dethlefsen, MEI's aquaprobed archaeologist.

He told me his story: his doctorate at Harvard in anthropology, his growing disillusionment through 20 years of teaching; his excitement at meeting with Clifford; his decision to write MEI's archaeological plan; his resignation as president of the Society for Historical Archaeology; his discovery that everything Clifford had ever told him was a lie; and his final swim to the beach from the *Vast Explorer*.

Immediately afterward, the archaeologist wrote a history of the wreck called *Whidah: Cape Cod's Mystery Ship*. He took copies to the Cape to sell in front of the Land Ho restaurant in Orleans but gave up when his colleague, another archaeologist, got a tap on the shoulder and a fist in the face from Clifford.

"I was literally ill for the next two or three years," Dethlefsen said, shaking his head. "I had not only destroyed my career; I had destroyed my confidence in having a career. I've been out of it since then. Life is too short."

The archaeologist walked me out to my rental car, where I dug out copies of *The Shell Game* and my *New Yorker* piece for him. Meanwhile, he inscribed my copy of his *Whydah* book and promised to send me his notes from his time among the pirates.

"Treasure hunters call me fairly often," he said. "They want to use my name as a scientist so they can get investors, and they offer me a percentage. One guy said he has a galleon in the Gulf worth a billion dollars." The archaeologist almost laughed, but couldn't shake the bitterness. "A billion dollars!" He shook his head. "The guy offered me one percent. He brought his wife and mother-in-law for display purposes. The treasure hunters don't want to learn anything. They just see gold."

"What do *you* say?"

The archaeologist sighed. "All I ask is a contract and a retainer up front."

I shook his hand, got in the rental car, and made it about three blocks before I had to pull off the road. I knew somehow that Dethlefsen wasn't long for this world, and I couldn't see through the tears.

I read his inscription:

*Best Wishes to Steve, who
will write a better book.*

That evening my wife and I flew back to New York, and Clifford called me from Orleans. There was a widow on the Cape, he said. Her bankers met with him. They agreed on a deal to buy shares of his stock. They were looking forward to reading my book.

I felt a pain in my gut like an ulcer.

With Bernstein and Betts, I had laughed at the fleecing of Heafitz. With Charlie Burnham, I had chuckled about Dethlefsen swimming ashore. With Rob Reedy, I had chortled about Riess' cofferdam. With Todd Murphy, I had joked about Frank Wells' dive to Disneyland. And as a journalist, I had laughed at them all. What a riotous bunch of scoundrels and suckers. But Clifford was ahead of me all the time. He had even been honest about it. He told me up front that he was more dangerous than a tiger shark. He dressed like a fisherman and carried a rod in the shape of a rolled-up *New York Times*. He'd used all the classic baits: vanity, greed, lust, jealousy. And I had swallowed them all—thinking I was playing him. My credentials sold *The Pirate Prince*. Now those same credentials were selling stock to some widow on Cape Cod.

Clifford knew that I was about to start writing. He must have figured it was time to give a little tug on the line.

That same night I set to work writing a chronology for *The Pirate Prince*—the rough borders of the picture my puzzle pieces would eventually fill. I planned to expose him, humiliate him, destroy him. He would strap himself with dynamite, give a final howl, and fall on the plunger.

But as the days went by my anger ebbed. Clifford didn't destroy the archaeologist. Clifford only enabled the archaeologist to destroy himself. If the mysterious widow had bankers who got her into a treasure hunt, then she had money to burn. Maybe the widow didn't even exist. I wasn't afraid of being beaten up by Clifford. No, I assured myself. It was just that I had no real proof of anything. "Your Honor, *Exhibit A* is a mat of mung located twenty feet under sand about a quarter mile off Marconi Beach. If the court would be so kind as to put on scuba gear and dig till we find it again, this mung mat will prove that Mr. Clifford is in fact a pirate."

All I would need to complete my prosecution was Mat Costa's black patch.

Then I pulled out my contract with the book packager and noticed paragraph 10:

> Writer shall not permit or arrange for the
> publication, distribution, or sale of any work which
> will compete with the Work or diminish the value
> of any subsidiary or additional rights granted by this
> agreement.

If I failed to write a book acceptable to Lief, the packager could fire me, demand his money back, and sue me if I tried to write anything contrary. Trapped, I finally sat down to write a prologue. The incident had seemed a joke at the time. Now it seemed a perfect excuse for whatever came next:

> Reality shifts when you're looking down the blade of a long knife. Of course the man crouched before you wielding it is fooling. The pirates were drowned or hanged long ago. Their ship has been found, and their treasure brought up and stowed in a vault at the Chatham branch of the Bank of New England. You're in a modern Cape Cod kitchen, and you're pretty sure this knife has never cut anything more substantial than a carrot. Still, you wonder.
> Barry Clifford, the fellow who found the pirate ship, straightens up and winks one of his wide blue eyes. "If somebody comes at you with the blade toward you like this, don't worry. The guy doesn't know what he's doing."
> Clifford flipped the handle over in his palm and cocked his wrist so the blade disappeared along the inside of his arm. "There. Now you can't see it. If I just wave my other hand to distract you, you haven't got a chance."
> His body tensed, distracted by some thought that took his eyes far away. Then he shrugged. He flipped his wrist and the knife sailed about six feet and sank to the hilt into the flank of a Styrofoam coffee cup propped up in the garbage can.
> He retrieved the knife. "Where do you suppose we should start this book?" he asked.

Their Ship Came In . . .
and Sank Them

On the morning of January 24, 1990, the phone rang in my office. I saved the file on my computer, clicked on the printer, and picked up the receiver. "Steve Kiesling."

"Hey, Steve Kiesling, We need to talk."

"Okay. Who's this?"

"Rob McClung. I'm at the Helmsley Palace on Madison. I'm free this evening. How 'bout dinner?"

I lay the receiver on my desk and stared at it. My stomach knotted. Shit! I picked up the receiver.

"You there?" McClung was saying.

"Yeah, sorry. Just dropped something. What brings you to town?"

"Financing a treasure hunt in the Bahamas. You might find it interesting." McClung paused. I didn't fill the gap. "You write for *Sports Illustrated*? Anyway, I thought you wanted to talk to me about the *Whydah*."

"Yeah," I said finally. "Where and when?"

"The bar here. I've got a meeting this afternoon, so why don't we confirm around five?"

McClung gave me the number and hung up.

I grabbed the hard copy from the printer and walked out of my office—through the dining room, the living room and out onto the front terrace. Even in winter I often paced the tiles, reading aloud from whatever I had written. But now there was no room. Giant hoists had been set up to support a platform for the men repairing the building's facade. The iron railing had been taken down. Beyond the hoist was a sheer drop of 18 floors to the scaffolding over the sidewalk. I leaned against one of the hoists and looked down, watching the flow of cars along 79th Street. I felt sick.

It's what happens when rage burns out.

Fear.

The steel and glass tower of the Helmsley Palace Hotel soars 54 stories behind the facade of some gilded Florentine-Renaissance-style townhouses built in the 1890s by Henry Villard, a journalist with a flair for hyperbole who ended up as president of the Northern Pacific railroad. The place seemed appropriate for a treasure deal—especially now that Leona Helmsley, "Queen of the Palace," was under indictment for tax fraud. I arrived at the hotel wearing my tweed jacket with the elbow patches, and it also felt appropriate. I was an undergraduate with finals looming who wanted desperately to go home.

The Helmsley bar—Villard's music room—was up two flights of grand marble stairs. The music room may also have been grand once, but it had become so tacky that Leona had turned off the lights. I couldn't see when I entered. Then I froze. At the bar with his back to me was Barry Clifford. Hatless! His scalp gleamed in the dim light. He turned slowly, and I recognized it was McClung. They could have been twins. But when we shook hands his green eyes didn't waver. If McClung was going to lie to me, he would do it even better than Clifford.

McClung tossed down the remainder of his beer, and we left the Helmsley and walked up Madison Avenue toward a Japanese restaurant. The night was clear and cold, and the city seemed deserted. He started talking about his current venture.

"One needs to know the right people to get a salvage permit in the Bahamas," McClung was saying. "So my partners and I hired an attorney who was a member of the parliament. That got us a meeting with the minister of transportation, and we flew down. Everything was going great until I noticed a map on the wall outlining permits already granted. Our spot was taken. It was as if someone knew exactly where we wanted to go."

I started to smile, but caught myself. What level of game was this?

"The minister was sympathetic," McClung continued. "Said he knew the owner of the permit and would introduce us on our next visit to the Bahamas. It took an hour to convince the minister to just call the guy. Then he picks up the phone and says 'George' like the guy is in the next room."

"Coincidence?" I asked.

"Who knows? We made a deal that day. George owns a marina and a bunch of hotels. He lives in the house where *Thunderball* was filmed—the one with the shark pools."

I laughed. "This sounds like a story after all. What boat are you using?"

"A 165-footer called *Oceanic Explorer.*

"Formerly *Maritime Explorer?*"

"Yeah."

"Who put up the money?"

"The guy who owns the boat. Bruce Heafitz. You heard of him?"

"Yeah," I said, chuckling inwardly, wondering how many times this Harvard man could be fleeced.

Inside the restaurant the treasure hunter gasped at the price of sushi: twenty-six bucks for a few ounces of raw tuna. Nevertheless, he was buying, and I wasn't going to fight for it. As we waited for drinks, the former police chief related a coincidence in Aspen.

"Clifford was visiting, and we were skiing with friends when we ran into Ethel Kennedy with an entourage of kids. I introduced Clifford, and it didn't take long before he was off skiing with the kids. The Kennedys were leaving the following day, and Clifford made me promise to phone him when they came back.

"That spring, the Secret Service called me to say that Ted Kennedy (then a candidate for President) was coming. So I called Clifford, and he flew out.

"Clifford was beside himself when he saw Ted on the slopes. As soon as I introduced him, Clifford leaped ahead of the Secret Service to get onto the chair lift. Then he skied some more with the kids. When Clifford went back to the Vineyard, he kept asking the kids out on his boat."

"How do you know that?" I asked.

"Because they called me to ask if Clifford was straight."

The sushi arrived quickly and was gone even faster. We left early and hungry. We returned to the dark bar at the Helmsley, took stools at the far corner, and ate goldfish crackers over beers. I scrounged sheets of loose note paper from the bartender and folded them in half lengthwise. McClung watched.

"You're not what I expected," he said.

"How so?"

"For one thing, most reporters carry tape recorders. At least notepads."

I was fishing through my jacket pockets for a pen and finally found one. *"Voila!"* I said "Armed and dangerous." I put the pen down. "Tape recorders just make it easier to make things up. If I don't use one, I have to be damn sure I write what you really mean to say."

McClung considered this, and we both arrived at the same conclusion. "I guess that's bullshit," I said. "I don't use tape recorders because they always break on me, and because I hate listening to my own voice." I took a sip of beer. "The real reason is, I didn't think you'd talk for the record." I picked up my pen. "Why did you call?"

"I wasn't going to," McClung replied. "I didn't want to have anything to do with your book, but Clifford called me the other day. He heard about the Bahamas deal with Heafitz and went apeshit. Said he was going to smear me in the book."

McClung looked for a moment like somebody had died.

"You liked him a lot?"

"He was my best friend. He always told stories. First day we met he told me his father was a Harvard attorney. In Aspen he always wanted me to introduce him as a photographer for *National Geographic*. It used to be funny. He didn't used to believe himself." McClung scowled. "Now he's just a salvor of other people's stories. I guess that's what happens when you don't have an identity of your own."

"But he did find the *Whydah*."

McClung snorted. "He was on shore when most of the finding was going on."

"Sure. But Clifford knew where to stake the claim. It wasn't Southack's map. I'm sure of that. I also know he didn't use Sam Harding's house like he told Cronkite. Clifford didn't start looking for Harding's house until after he filed for the permit. Frankly, I just don't get it. However he did it, he applied for a permit in exactly the right place."

McClung was shaking his head. "He read the sign."

"What?"

"On the cliff." McClung started to chuckle. "You didn't know this? A long time ago the National Park Service put up a sign about the *Whydah* next to the Marconi model. Clifford showed me the sign and said, 'When I came to the beach to think about where to apply, basically all I did was look at this sign. They had to put it here for some reason.'"

McClung shrugged. "The sign was right in line with the wreck. After we found the wreck, the Park Service took down the sign. I have a picture of it somewhere."

I sat back on my stool and tried to collect my thoughts. The story was so completely stupid, it had to be true. "Okay, let met get this straight. Clifford reads the sign on the beach: *Wreck Thataway!* But he doesn't look closely at the Marconi station model, and so he doesn't realize that the beach in 1717 was a thousand feet farther out. Then Clifford and Mel Fisher go out with a magnetometer and find the radio tower. Clifford uses those mag readings along with some nails from Martha's Vineyard to get a permit—which he brings to Aspen to raise money."

McClung nodded. "That's essentially right."

"Then you dig up the radio tower, which became mizzen stays and rudder straps. The next year the erosion problem gets sorted out, and you dive down and find the cannons—right where the sign says. Then the archaeologist Warren Riess shows up with his cofferdam. He spends weeks and thousands of dollars to dig one tiny pit, so you guys say 'screw the archaeologists,' and start digging on your own."

McClung was shaking his head. "No."

"Bullshit. I saw the mats of mung. More pits were dug than the archaeologists know about."

McClung wasn't smiling. "Sure. But they were dug before Riess got there. We opened up the entire impact area."

"You found the wreck and just started blowing?"

"Yeah. We figured we should at least take a look before turning it over to the archaeologists."

"How many pits could you dig in a day?"

"On a calm day, a dozen. On a lousy day, two or three. Three or four or five was the average. If you don't believe me, check the '83 Annual Report. According to the report we dug only seven pits that season, but the report also explains that each pit had as many as forty overlapping holes. The state specified the number of pits we could dig, but not the number of holes."

"So a single pit could be as big as a battleship, depending on how many holes were in it." This sounded like a concept from Philosophy 110 at Yale.

"That's the way it worked out." McClung agreed. "Except for the bell the next year, every large artifact that has ever been found on the site was mapped that first season. We found about forty cannons, although some got counted more than once. We could have brought up everything that year, but there was no lab to put it in."

"Were the artifacts on different layers?"

"Originally, yeah. The wreck was on different planes. The

more we blew the more everything settled to the same plane. We homogenized the wreck. We also pushed a lot of stuff way down—out of reach. The original wreck was under eight to ten feet of sand. We blew it to twenty feet."

"Did Warren Riess know?"

"Not the full extent of it. Clifford said at first that we would turn over all the maps to the archaeologists, but then he decided to destroy most of them. He wanted it to seem like all the coins came out of one small pit, and that the rest of the site had never been touched."

McClung sighed: "Archaeology? You could forget about it."

"Did Bernstein and Betts know?"

"They were so greedy they hardly knew anything," said McClung. His tone was morose, but then his eyes lit up. "It's funny. The bell was last significant artifact we found, and it's what convinced them to do the stock offering." He chuckled. "Of course, they knew enough not to trust Clifford."

"What do you mean?"

"Before the deal could be sold to investors, it first had to be sold to Hutton's regional brokers. That meeting was in Denver, and Clifford was in New York."

"So who presented the offering to Hutton's brokers?"

"I did," McClung replied. "I slipped up once, and somebody asked me about the number of cannons. But the brokers would have bought anything. They kept saying 'are you sure six million is enough?' They said they could raise fifteen million easy."

McClung gave a wan smile. "Forty percent of the stock was bought by people at E.F. Hutton."

There was a moral in that somewhere, but it wasn't the time to sort out what it might be. Meanwhile, McClung was running his hand over his scalp, looking forlorn. "I feel weird telling you all this," he said. "It sounds like I was an accomplice or something. I kept thinking it was going to get better. That Clifford would stop lying. But it kept getting worse. It was a nightmare you couldn't wake up from."

I gathered up my papers and folded them into my jacket pocket, and we left the bar. We walked together down the marble stairs and shook hands in the lobby.

"You think there's treasure still out there?" I asked.

"If there was treasure there, I would be digging it." He turned away, heading for the bank of elevators.

Quite a long time after my evening with McClung I would begin to wonder about Clifford's chance meeting with the Kennedys in Aspen—and their subsequent scuba dives together off Martha's Vineyard. Those events occurred at about the same time—the end of the seventies. It was also about that time that Clifford began to talk about the *Whydah*. Clifford's log suggested a connection:

> I thought how odd some of the circumstances are surrounding the project—for instance the Kennedy involvement. 1. John F. K. Sr. was extremely interested in the National Seashore. Jackie's nephew found coins on the beach presumed from the *Whidah*. Jackie's interest in calling me ect. John's interest in asking me for a job, finally the fact the there were Kennedys aboard the *Mary Ann* when she wrecked.

The *Mary Anne* was one of Bellamy's final prizes, the cargo ship filled with wine. She ran aground in the storm, and her men—three of her original crew and seven pirates—gathered in her hold to say to their prayers and drink themselves into oblivion. Much to their surprise, however, they awoke on dry land. Soon exposed as pirates, they were captured. They broke free but were too hung over to get away.

So far as I know, no Kennedys were aboard the *Mary Anne* the night she hit the beach. But there was a likeable Irish lad, a 19-year-old member of the original crew, Tom Fitzgerald. Fitzgerald was captured along with the pirates. When they escaped, he feared revenge from the sheriff and went with them. As a result the young Irishman sat in a Boston jail from May till October, when the pirates' trial cleared him.

I haven't asked, but perhaps there is some special resonance between Tom Fitzgerald and John Fitzgerald Kennedy. And if this story—or something like it—is true, the search for the *Whydah* may have been in part Clifford's way of sinking a hook deep into the Kennedy clan.

But I wasn't that crazy yet. At least I wasn't thinking along those lines. And so, after I left McClung at the hotel, I went back to my apartment and did what I could to check out his version of the discovery of the *Whydah*. From the Cape Cod National Seashore Information Bureau, I learned that an exhibit called Famous Shipwrecks had been at the observation area at Marconi Beach until it was retired in 1984. Knowing what to look for, I noticed the following in Ted Dethlefsen's book:

> Some years ago the National Park Service placed on the cliff above the Wellfleet beach a bronze tablet that says the wreck is right there offshore. The cliff overlooks the beach where most of the old Spanish coins have been found. Long after Bellamy and his ship were lost, people claimed to see portions of her sticking out of a sand bar after storms had shifted and reshaped immense masses of sea bottom...

After working through the ancient clues to the wherabouts of the wreck, Clifford's first archaeologist concluded:

> The wreck should have occurred, therefore, approximately where the Park Service tablet says it did.

Like the *"General Arnold"* sticking out of the mud in Plymouth Harbor, the location of the *Whydah* must have seemed obvious: Clifford probably just read the sign.

He might then have asked somebody to explain the inscription on the sign: *A pirate treasure of £20,000 apparently went down...*

And he might have been told twenty-thousand "pounds."

Had Clifford studied the Marconi radio station model—about fifty yards away—he might then have calculated the rate of erosion and found the *Whydah* in a weekend.

Before Clifford came along, most Cape Codders figured that the wreck had been picked over for centuries. And obviously it had been. Nevertheless, the soup of sand off Marconi Beach held enough coins to make a small venture worthwhile. It might have stayed small if Clifford hadn't imposed the media black out and taken his pail of artifacts to the chairman of Random House. Robert Bernstein set in motion the Media Plan, which put Clifford on the cover of *Parade*. From there to Cronkite...

Oddly enough, America's anchorman stuck his nose into one of the biggest clues of the story. As the credits rolled Cronkite was down on all fours on the deck of the *Vast Explorer*, sniffing the barrel of a cannon with the enthusiasm of a young collie. "Take a look right here," Cronkite gushed. "That's air coming out of that barrel. Isn't that incredible! That's the air those guys were breathing the last moment of their lives. I'm breathing two-hundred-and-seventy-year-old air. Isn't that amazing!"

If he hadn't been doing a favor for the chairman of Random House, Cronkite might have sniffed more critically and learned that the air from the cannon was probably gas bubbles from the barnacles.

Cronkite might also have read Dethlefsen's book—and thought twice about announcing "tons of gold, silver, indigo, and ivory" or a $6 million stock offering. According to the archaeologist:

> If the treasure was in coinage, and if the coins
> are still in good condition, it might be worth in the
> neighborhood of 4 or 5 million today.

Still the puzzle made no sense. Why raise six million dollars to dig up areas you've dug up already? Why buy a new ship that's too big for the site?

Those questions started me digging through my files again—to the very first packet of information from Phillip Lief.

Eureka!

On April 30, 1987, as E.F. Hutton's deal went down and the great ship *Maritime Explorer* was bought, Senator Edward Kennedy wrote a letter to the President of the Azores to "once again reiterate my strong endorsement for this outstanding and committed team of underwater archaeologists led by Mr. Barry Clifford and his company."

Clifford was going global. And his best hope for a real $100 million treasure trove were some Spanish galleons in deep water off the Azores. Treasure hunters weren't allowed in the Azores. A salvage permit could require a lot of money, connections, and a very big ship:

Six million dollars, Ted Kennedy, and the *Maritime Explorer,* for example.

Tin Men

"Whydah Partners was all wrapped up in moviedom," Bruce Heafitz said. "They told Barry how they were going to make him the next Harrison Ford. He told them all he was going to find. They totally fed on each other. They finally got to believing each other. In a way they deserved it."

"It's like two girls going to the prom each telling the other the other one is prettier, only to find out that someone else is crowned queen of the prom."

And who's going to be queen of the prom?

"I am," said Heafitz. "I want to be the prettiest girl at the prom."

— *Cape Cod Times,* July 19, 1989

I can't remember now the score of the Super Bowl in 1990. I don't even remember who played. But I do remember my stroke in the Gillette commercial. It aired during the pregame show, the first quarter, halftime, and the fourth quarter. Witnessed by more people than any other rowing stroke in the history of the universe, it paid at an hourly rate of about $334,800. So successful was the commercial that it would be pulled off the air because Gillette couldn't keep up with the demand. Even so, my half-second contribution would flash for about eight minutes worldwide and pay about $45,328— some $328 more than my contract for *The Pirate Prince*.

Those whom the Gods will cut to pieces they first buy plenty of razor blades.

There were intimations of what was to come. I was working full time at my word processor but getting nowhere— falling further behind on the deadline. Only seven weeks remained. Meanwhile, my editor at the Phillip Lief Group left the company for philosophical reasons that sounded like an archaeologist talking about a treasure hunter. Then Lief phoned to say that he would edit the manuscript himself. Like a shrink or a lover, an editor can awaken powers and possibilities you never imagined—or he can lop off your arm or blow off your kneecap just to let you know he's there.

I knew what to expect.

Nevertheless, I was still the game—determined not to lose by default. And so on March 12, 1990, I met my agent outside the grime-colored lobby on West 20th Street and rode with him in the slow, grinding elevator to the offices of the Phillip Lief Group. I wore a business suit and contact lenses. I carried an English leather satchel. At the sound of the buzzer I strutted into Lief's office under a mantle of righteous rage. Lief looked wrinkled and unpolished. The circles under his eyes looked like glasses. He had a new baby, he explained.

I pulled a file folder from my satchel and spread two diagrams on the coffee table.

The Pirate Prince
July 1989

Prentice Hall

Phillip Lief
47.5% of movie

Clifford—story	Kiesling—writer
47.5% of movie	5% of movie

The Pirate Crook
March 1990

Prentice Hall

Phillip Lief
13.5% of movie rights

Whydah Management
85% of movie rights

Clifford—lies	Kiesling—reporter
	1.5% of movie

"Just look at these," I told Lief. "Clifford didn't own the rights to *The Pirate Prince,* and yet he signed a deal with you. Bernstein and Betts should have known Clifford was peddling *their* book, but they didn't step in until after you sold it to Prentice Hall. Why?"

"They must know that the true story could sink them. I can't believe they really want this book."

Lief looked as if he was having a baby. I kept going. "You know what they're like, Phillip. They screwed us out of the movie rights."

"Who told you that?" Lief snapped.

"I'm a reporter, remember?"

"You weren't supposed to know about that."

"Thanks," I said, and got going again, a hundred degrees hotter. "The Wall Streeters told me to check Clifford's stories with three other sources. Why? They're not stupid. They just can't admit Clifford beat them. Turns out that Tom Bernstein was going through a divorce during the Hutton deal. That explains a lot of this."

I had begun to babble, but kept on. It didn't help that I had told Lief much of the real *Whydah* story back in January. Before I met McClung, I still thought I could somehow write the book in the contract.

"Listen," I said. *"The Pirate Crook* is a much better story. And we can pull it off. I'll need until Labor Day to write it, more money for the extra time—say twenty thousand—and indemnification in case Clifford sues me."

Lief stared out the window. He looked exhausted. The new baby...

March, February, January, December, November, October, September, August, July... *Oh shit!*

The child and *The Pirate Prince* had been conceived about the same time—and Lief had allowed me the same gestation period. The book must have seemed a gift from the gods.

I was threatening his child.

Lief composed himself. "Why do I keep hearing these stories?" he said, his voice like iron on velvet. "Why am I not reading them?"

"I'm not that far along."

"What?"

"I can't get too much further until I get the maps. That's why I need until Labor Day."

"You're waiting for *maps?"*

Finally, Lief was getting it, I thought.

"That's what I've been telling you. McClung drew maps of everything ever found on the site three years before Hutton's stock offering. Clifford wanted them destroyed, but McClung saved the originals in his attic. At least he says he did. The maps prove that this whole thing is a scam. It's kind of funny. Last summer, at the very beginning of the project, I was at McClung's house. I ate dinner right underneath the mother lode."

Thinking about it now I almost chuckled. "As soon as McClung gets back from the Bahamas, he's going to give me the maps."

Lief's stare was long and venomous enough for me to re-think what I had just said, feel like an idiot, and get mad all over again.

"Frankly," he snarled, "I don't know who the pirate is: Clifford or you, Mr. Kiesling."

My shoulders shook. My eyes welled up. I could barely talk. "You...*fucking*...don't...understand. We are *in* this thing. Right now Clifford says he is using this book to sell stock to little old ladies on Cape Cod. Either we stop him or we help him."

Lief maintained an icy calm, which made me angrier still. He stopped the meeting long enough to bring in one of his assistants to act as a witness, but mostly he let me rant until I blew out.

Miraculously, my agent smoothed things over. We all wanted the same thing, he said. A good book. Lief said the extra time and money was possible and that he could deal with Clifford. In turn, I left Lief with about a hundred pages of rough manuscript. As we rode down the elevator my agent looked at me and shook his head.

"The good cop/bad cop routine worked pretty well," he

said. "But this was first time in my career that I got to play the good cop."

Two weeks later, on Wednesday, March 28, I was at my word processor, struggling with Sam Bellamy's career in the Bahamas, when the phone rang. I found myself holding for Mr. Roland Betts. He came on the line bright and cheerful. He asked how things were going. Fine. He seemed surprised.

"Why'd you quit?" Betts asked.

"Where did you hear that?"

"Phillip Lief told Tom that you were uncomfortable and had resigned."

"I am uncomfortable, but quitting is news to me."

"Well, you can't write a fantasy," Betts said.

"I'm glad you feel that way." I replied, and I was. "What else did Lief say?

Betts was silent for a moment. "It sounds like I've stepped in the middle of something," he said finally. "A friend of mine is at Prentice Hall. I'll give her a call and find out what's going on."

Betts hung up. I dialed my agent.

"Lief is saying I've quit. Know anything about it?"

"Maybe. I'm expecting a messenger from Lief this afternoon. I'll fax it as soon as it comes."

The day wore on with no word from my agent. I called back, but the messenger had not arrived. I then phoned Lief's office and learned that he was at home tending his baby. He returned the call an hour or so later. I felt almost jovial when I heard his voice.

"Hey Phillip, I hear I've been fired."

"That's right." Lief sounded surprised that I knew, but not disappointed.

"Thank god! You gonna get another writer?"

"I'm working on it."

"A race to the bookshelves then! It'll sell more for both of us."

That got a rise. "When you read the letter from my attorney, I expect you'll give up that idea." Buried in Lief's anger was confidence. He had something.

Two days passed before Lief's messenger arrived at my agent's office. By then I had cleaned my office four or five times and spilled most of a beer into my fax machine. My agent's cover letter gurgled through with more than the usual slurring of thermal ink. All my agent wrote was, *"You're not going to believe this."*

The fax vomited up a few sentences of Lief's attorney's letter before the machine beeped plaintively and died. From what I could read, my demands for more time, money, and protection "constituted a fundamental breach" of my contract to deliver a "proper autobiographical work," whatever that was. If I did not give "prompt reassurance" that I would deliver such a work by the agreed date and at the agreed price, I would be held liable.

The fax sputtered back to life.

...it appears that you have obtained a great deal of information from Mr. Clifford, from Whydah Joint Venture and its affiliates, and from others, based on the misrepresentation that you were writing a proper autobiographical book as required by the agreement. All of the circumstances, including the nature and extent of your interviews, indicate that you have known for a long time (if not from the beginning) that you planned to give a critical "investigative" twist to this book, at variance with the requirements of the agreement... We must therefore insist upon your assurance that, apart from the work you are

writing for PLG...you will not write or publish, or
assist anyone else to write or publish any work about
Mr. Clifford or *Whydah* and its affiliates or any other
work based on what you have obtained from them
or with their cooperation....

When the buzzer rang from the lobby a few minutes later,
I was still sprawled across my chair like an entomologist's
display. The buzzer heralded Matthew, who was coming up
with his bicycle. Matthew had rowed with me at Yale and
was my pair partner in the '84 Olympic trials. Now my closest friend, he was a writer for the daytime soaps. He understood these things. He came into my office stripping off cy-
cling gloves, and I handed him the letter.

Matthew began to read and to rumble. He's about six-foot-
seven and has a deep rumble like a train in a tunnel. "Ooohh
Errrr oohh. This is not good. You're going to wake up some
morning itching like crazy. You'll roll over and discover your
sheets are covered with fiberglass dust and lying beside you
hacked off is the bow of your single scull."

"That bad?"

"Worse. This either came from a *consigliori* or a Harvard
lawyer. Maybe both."

"You're not making me feel any better."

"Steve, it's time to bail on this one. But there is one good
thing. If you were making up this stuff, they wouldn't write
this letter. They're sitting on a turd." Matthew rolled the fax
paper back into a tube and tossed it like a dart toward the pile
on my desk. "Come on, let's ride."

"You think I'll get those maps?"

"I didn't before. Have you heard from that guy McClung?"

"I left a message for him in West Palm Beach. I figure he's
in the Bahamas. You think I should go down there? He in-

vited me."

"Out in the middle of the ocean scuba diving with Clifford's former best friend? You outta your mind?"

"You're right. I am going to Aspen. I gotta do that. And my friend the Smithsonian director, Roger Kennedy, has got a new place at Keystone. It'll work out."

"Shoot yourself."

The store front office of the *Aspen Times* has a clippings library and a coin-operated photocopier. I requested the police files from '82 and '83 and then dropped a pile of change on top of the copier. I intended to copy everything and read it later, but I was soon hooked by the stories. I read that McClung had been an exceptional skier. In '83, Aspen's Police ski team won the state and national titles. McClung placed 12th out of 117 racers from 30 agencies and then went on to the police ski team World Championships. I also learned that Chief McClung ran for sheriff and was "thumped" in the primaries by a "dove" opposed to undercover drug raids.

The case of the missing pistol made the paper several times. On March 31, 1983, the District Attorney was quoted as saying, "The contents of a 30-page report prepared by the Colorado Bureau of Investigation made it clear that either McClung was lying or that everyone else in the department who spoke with investigators was not telling the truth." On April 7, the same reporter wrote, "The credibility of Aspen's police department has fallen to levels usually reserved for used-car salesmen, weathermen, and Pentagon cost estimators." Eleven days later, the *Times* reported McClung's resignation.

I didn't feel well.

I gathered up my photocopies, left the *Times,* and almost got run over crossing the street into the shopping plaza below the ski slopes. What a mess! Did I believe in McClung's maps for the same reason investors believed in Clifford's mother lode? Was I on a witch hunt? Was that the flip side of a treasure hunt? I sat on the curb in the bright spring sun, watching the skiers hurtling downward, thinking I was going mad.

Two days later, on cross-country skis near Keystone, I formulated a new plan. Roger Kennedy and I would convene a meeting at the Yale Club in Manhattan. There, beneath the *Lux et Veritas* banner, I would reveal everything I knew. In front of the Smithsonian director, they wouldn't threaten me or even offer to buy my silence. Although the story made them look stupid, the scandal could boost the value of their treasure and help them to pay off their investors.

But Kennedy shook his head. "First, you'll need to secure all the evidence, write an explanation, put the originals in a safe-deposit box, and give copies to an attorney.

"It sounds so melodramatic, but people have disappeared for less."

I was living a B movie.

Meanwhile, my agent worked to patch things up in New York, and he relayed fragments of various conversations. Except for Clifford, the parties concerned had read the draft manuscript and decided that the central character was, to use Lief's description, "despicable." Everyone agreed that I was not writing the book they desired. They wanted a "puff piece."

"Can you do it?" My agent asked.

"I don't know. I guess so. The contract says I need to make a good faith effort, so I'll try. But first we need to sit down with everybody and let them figure out how to tell this story."

"I'm sure we can arrange that," my agent said. "I'll get back to you."

When my agent phoned again he said there would be a meeting the following Wednesday. Lief, Betts, Bernstein, and

Marilyn Abraham from Prentice Hall would all attend. Unfortunately, we were not invited.

"Their problem isn't Clifford," my agent said. "It's you."

I remember wondering if I was going to be fired that Wednesday afternoon. I wanted desperately to be fired. They had to kill the book. After Aspen, I didn't know what to believe. I just wanted out. Thinking they were meeting for lunch, I stayed near the phone, but the afternoon wore on without word. It wasn't until evening that Lief called.

"We're going to give you another chance," he said. "Write a fresh chapter. We're not asking you to whitewash the story, but you need to change the tone."

"The tone?"

"Steve, this is for your own good. No one would want to read the book you're writing. But if you get the right tone, you should be able to use most if not all of your material."

"What about the deadline?"

"If you succeed, we'll extend it till Labor Day and pay you for the extra time. I've hired a new editor. You'll like her. She went to Yale."

"Okay. When do I get to sit down with everybody to talk this thing through?"

"That's not going to happen. You're suffering from too many bosses. That's been my fault. In the future you will speak to no one other than me or your editor here. You don't have a moment to waste."

Lief hung up, and I phoned Tom Bernstein. He took the call only to say there was nothing more to discuss. I stood in my kitchen with tears of anger and frustration rolling down my face, unable to speak. I managed to spit out that I didn't want to become "an accessory to stock fraud."

"That's a very large accusation," Bernstein replied. "You agreed to write a book that's acceptable. Are you reneging on that?"

With a word the game could have been over. In time I would have stopped twitching at the recollection. But I couldn't somehow. "No, Tom. I'm not a lawyer. I guess I don't know what words like accessory mean."

"Don't be so naive. If you were hired to write a book about Ted Kennedy you wouldn't expect to write about Chappaquiddick."

Four days before the contract deadline, on April 27, I sent Lief a draft of a new chapter—"The Chutzpah Factor"—about Mel Fisher and the first "discovery" of the *Whydah*. It seemed an innocuous part of the tale, and I did my best to climb into Clifford's head—to see the adventure through his eyes. It felt good to write, but I also felt like I was building a scab over the truth. And that did not feel good at all.

But it worked. Sort of. Lief said he would extend the deadline until Labor Day and pay for the time. But Lief also demanded to see a new version of Chapter One, immediately. So I wrote that and sent it in. I plowed ahead while it was read at Prentice Hall.

Two weeks went by without word, and the uncertainty gnawed. I didn't know what I was writing anymore. I had no idea where it was going. I needed time to think it through, and there wasn't any time. The deadline extension and the extra money were not in writing. I began calling my agent almost daily for news. There was none. By June 4, I was frantic. Without encouragement, I wouldn't finish by Labor Day. Not even by Christmas.

Figuring the gods needed an offering, I wrote a poem for Marilyn Abraham at Prentice Hall and enclosed with it an antique silver brooch in the shape of a galleon. The brooch once belonged to my grandmother. Costume jewelry, I think. I agonized about whether to send the gift and finally called a messenger.

The response was instantaneous. It sputtered out of my fax machine on letterhead from Lief's lawyer.

> This letter will confirm that you have not delivered the manuscript of the Book by the May 1, 1990 date required in the agreement.... In view of your material breach of the contract, our client demands immediate repayment of $25,000..."
>
> ...you must not write or publish, or assist anyone else to write or publish, any work about Mr. Clifford or *Whydah* or its affiliates or any other work based upon information that you have obtained from them or with their cooperation.... Unless the sum is repaid, we have been instructed to bring legal action to recover that sum, plus interest, and any and all damages that PLG has suffered as a result of your breach.

I called Abraham. "We needed to sit down and talk this thing through."

"I'm sorry," she said. "It's too late."

"But this whole thing is crooked. You really..."

She cut me off. "We have to move forward. Thanks for the brooch. It's very pretty. If you have any ideas to share for another book, I'd love to hear them."

At least Roland Betts sounded eager to get together. As soon as I hung up the phone with him, his secretary called me back with a meeting time. Because I remembered reading somewhere that power is in the hands of the person who sets the meeting, I called once more to change the time. Betts agreed, and so on the appointed day, I found my gold pocket watch, got my power suit from the cleaners, had my shoes shined, and then cooled my heels in his lobby for 45 minutes before he ushered me up to his penthouse.

So much for that.

Betts' jacket was off. The knot on his striped tie hung just below his open collar button. He offered me a seat on the sofa and then sat casually at his desk as if he might put his feet up. "Sorry about making you wait," he said. "You called this meeting?"

I looked at my hands, playing it weak because that's the way it was. Nevertheless, I had to play it that way to test my theory.

"It's boring watching somebody else learn that the world isn't what he thought it was," I began. "It's a lesson everybody has to learn, I guess. And now it's my turn." I shrugged deeper into his sofa. "I don't want to bore you, but I want to tell you what I've learned."

I looked up. Betts had his feet on the desk. It was a scene out of Payne Whitney gym at Yale—going to tell the coach that the boat didn't feel right. Being in the boat, I couldn't see all the oars, so there was always doubt. Maybe the coach was working on something bigger than whatever I felt through the seat of my shorts. But maybe he wasn't. And whose boat was it anyway? I would get all worked up, but all the coach had to do was pat me on the head, tell me that his plan was for the best, and I would go back and pull. My coach won a silver in '68, and mostly he was right.

So I told Betts what I knew of Clifford's story, starting with the ill fated *General Arnold* venture and the *Whydah* sign on the cliff. I told Betts that the mother lode had been mapped three years before Hutton's offering. No, I didn't have the maps. But I believed they had been made. It was pretty obvious.

All Betts had to do was acknowledge that we got stuck in the same mess, and that he knew the best way out. Betts could take my shirt. We'd shake hands, and it would be time to row back to the boathouse and buy some beer.

But Betts wouldn't admit anything—or even win gracefully. He pressed for sources. Whenever I mentioned one, he claimed to have heard a different story from the same person. Only six percent of the site had been excavated before Hutton came in. His only regret was failing to deal with the deep sand. If they had brought in a dredge to scoop away the top layer of sand, they would have uncovered a lot more treasure for a lot less money.

My neck went stiff. "You ever wonder why the sand kept getting deeper year after year?" I asked, my voice rising. "Because they were blowing the wreck to China. And what about your glorious flagship *Maritime Explorer*? Just bad luck that it was too big to float on the site?"

A direct hit.

Betts winced. His eyed tightened. He took his feet off the desk and thrust himself forward like a hockey star who has only seconds remaining in the penalty box. "Some deals go bad." he said. "How much money is at stake?"

I was thinking how different this meeting might have been if Betts had ridden the elevator to my penthouse, and I had greeted him in shorts and river-runner sandals. He would have sat on my sofa, admired my view, and understood that something else was at stake. But I had put on my power suit and shined my shoes. I looked and felt like a poor imitation of Roland Betts.

And so I set him up.

In the fifties, Betts learned about heroes from Walter

Cronkite. In the sixties Cronkite went to Viet Nam so Betts wouldn't have to. And at the peak of the eighties, Betts took control of the world's only pirate wreck, using Walter Cronkite to announce his stock.

How did Betts do it?

According to the prospectus, the *Whydah* offering was scheduled to close March 31 — the day after Cronkite's broadcast. So I have to believe that Cronkite scheduled his air date to break the news of the offering just as it closed. No harm done.

But Hutton's prospectus included the possibility of extending the close — and that's what happened. Betts extended the offering until May 28. The most trusted man in America gave everything but a 900 number hawking pirate stock nationwide.

It was just a game, of course. But still, why might Betts risk so much for something so stupid?

Why set up the man who introduced the heroes and helped save him from Viet Nam?

I think it was more than greed. More than hubris.

Revenge.

My theory is that a young hockey star named Roland Betts wanted to make the honorable choice in 1968 — and so he chose to become a teacher. But he wasn't Christ. And he hadn't made a sacrifice. He was only a young man — who, like most young men, desperately needed to prove himself to himself. Instead, he found himself hiding out. Rather than deal with it, he learned to lie.

Betts still winces at the recollection of when his heart was cut out. And he has been getting even ever since. His book *Acting Out* was about rage. He made a name for himself by financing *The Killing Fields* — a movie that heaped blame on

Richard Nixon while it tested a system that would be called "a whole new dimension in using other people's money."

It's just a theory, of course. But why else would the "best and brightest" of the most affluent and educated generation in the history of the world grow up to gut their schools and raid their fathers' pension funds to buy gold Rolex watches?

Betts' press release, *Pirate Partners Raise $6 Million,* said it all: "Recent Silver Screen film releases include the hits *Ruthless People, The Color of Money, Outrageous Fortune* and *Tin Men.*"

I looked at my hands. "I was paid twenty-five grand."

Betts barely suppressed a laugh. "We spent more than a year and over three million dollars on a new marketing plan for Silver Screen—and it flopped. You've got to learn to cut your losses." He sat back in his chair and clasped his hands behind his head, making a show of thinking.

"This is against my better judgment," he said. "But let me give you some legal advice. Lief doesn't have much of a case for getting his money back. You wrote quite a few pages and then made revisions. It would be hard to prove you didn't act in good faith."

Betts was smiling now. "If you were to write a letter to Lief and apologize—indicating that you weren't going to pursue this any further—you wouldn't have to pay back the advance. I can assure you of that."

Betts had handled the situation, and the meeting was over. He stood up. I followed his cue and headed toward the door. "Write the letter and walk away," he said. "It's that simple."

He opened the door for me and held out his hand. His voice dropped lower and became more intimate. "If you don't, I'll sue you. Phillip Lief will sue you. And Prentice Hall will sue you. We won't sue you for twenty-five grand. We'll sue for the value of the entire deal."

He patted me on the back, ushering me out.

"Don't make this a *cause celebre*," he said.

I left Betts' office, caught a subway to Times Square, and walked a few blocks to *The New Yorker*. I always hoped that Chip McGrath would take me to the Algonquin for lunch, but he always claimed to be tired of the place. That day, we went to one of those special Manhattan lunch spots where if you tilt your head you can take a bite out of somebody else's burger.

I had to admit that McGrath had been right all along about the project. He told me not to get involved. Getting fired was the best thing that could have happened to my career. While he was surprised that "Rolly" Betts had gotten himself into such a thing, he had no interest in publishing the story. It was not a profile and my role made it impossible. "A writer is only as good as his last published story," he said. "You've wasted one year of your life. Don't waste another."

"But Chip, the *Whydah* is being held up as proof that treasure hunters and archaeologists can work together for the good of everybody. What it actually proves is the opposite. That's important."

"If you have such a good case, go to the police. That's what they're for."

"A Harvard guy named Heafitz already tried. From what I hear, he got fleeced, and the DA laughed at him. Besides, we—the press—created Clifford. Robert Bernstein's Media Plan launched him. If we don't take Clifford out, we're just con men—like Janet Malcolm wrote. What was her lead? 'Every journalist who is not too stupid or too full of himself to notice what is going on knows that what he does is morally indefensible...'"

"Steve, this is not a big deal."

"Bullshit!" I stared at him wondering if he were right. Probably. He typically was. So what? "When we were at Alec's wedding last week, I talked to couple of young musicians at my table. They were from Provincetown, and they got together with some friends to buy stock from one of Clifford's divers, a guy named Scotty Magoun who lies about a shark bite. Magoun told them the wreck was worth a hundred million, and that he was giving them a special deal. Half the staff of *The New Yorker* was at that wedding. We're obligated to tell the story. Bernstein ought to buy the stock back."

McGrath looked exasperated. "We're not going to turn the magazine on its head for one writer with a vendetta. Jesus. I hope my son doesn't decide to row. You guys don't know when to quit. You've got to get something else going. Try it, will you?"

"Yeah, sure," I muttered.

When we parted, McGrath offered to find names of firms that specialized in literary law, and he called later that afternoon. He said the best was a firm famous for First Amendment cases. Then he gave me the name of the same lawyer who was threatening me on behalf of Phillip Lief.

I had to hand it to Clifford. He didn't even put up the retainer.

The Great White Tuna

By the middle of August 1990, I was freelancing again, on assignment for *Sports Illustrated*, crammed into the back seat of a tiny single-engine airplane headed out over Massachusetts Bay from Chatham. This was a different sort of treasure hunt—spotting giant bluefin tuna for harpoon fishermen—but a similar madness. One auction report from Great Circle Fisheries, which air freights tuna to Japan for *sushi*, explained it: Great Circle deducted a 16% Japanese commission, a 9% Stateside commission and more than a grand for air-freight, trucking, and packing. Even so, the return to the boat was about $15,000—of which the spotter pilot got 25%. Nearly $4,000 dollars for finding one fish.

And so the air space near Chatham had become like O'Hare without the control tower. As soon as one plane was "on fish," a dozen more would be weaving in and out of each other. The unofficial record was 20 spotter planes, stacked up at 50-foot intervals. The pilots talked to their boats using radios garbled by military-style scramblers, and their eyes were glued straight down. Sometimes they crashed. One hotshot died trying to herd a school of tuna.

On that particular day the other spotters of the Chatham squadron were grounded by the near-zero-visibility weather—and had been for almost a week. They spent their days hanging out on the balcony of the Crosswind Restaurant, fixated on the red warning light flashing between them and the single 3,000-foot runway. Meanwhile, the harpoon fleet was at sea, attempting to spot fish from their crow's nests, getting nothing. Everyone was going broke. And so, during a brief window in the fog, my pilot, the bull goose loony of this odd asylum, persuaded the rampdog to amble out of the hangar with his shotgun and scare the gulls off the runway. Within minutes, we were punching through patches of fog under a cloud ceiling of 500 feet.

I felt like Ishmael. My Ahab was a wiry, bent-nosed, and bowlegged cowboy named Freeman "Trip" Wheeler—Barry Clifford's third roommate at Western State College.

Wheeler's father was a fighter pilot who augered in. His stepfather was also a fighter pilot. At Western State, Wheeler washed out of Navy flight school for being untrainable, and so ended up in the Army. He taught himself to fly. Wheeler always wanted to fly in combat, and he got his chance in the early eighties, flying Air America style to Nicaragua and El Salvador. In his spare time he rode bulls in the rodeo. He dove for the *Whydah* during the '83 and '85 seasons.

He now rented Rob McClung's house in Chatham.

"Hot damn! Will you check that out!" It was Wheeler's voice through the earphones. As he spoke he banked hard to starboard, flipping the wing perpendicular to the water so that we were suspended on our seatbelts above a door that had

been removed for better spotting. Wheeler's left hand worked the stick, holding us in a tight spiral while his right hand pointed.

"Eleven o'clock!" The water rushed up as we spiraled down until it was like flying inside a washing machine just above the suds. "Coming out of the glare, right... *Now!"*

"What the hell is that?"

"It's the great albino tuna."

A cowboy pilot telling a fish story. "I don't need this."

"Look!"

It didn't look like a shark or a whale or a porpoise or a flatfish. It looked like a great white tuna. Moby tuna.

Maybe it was!

Then it vanished. Wheeler leveled the wings and pulled back on the stick. "Whenever I see that fish there's no boat close enough to do anything about it. But it's a good omen."

A few minutes later we gave up on the Bay and headed east over the Cape toward the Atlantic. We followed Southack's whaleboat route across Jeremiah's Gutter into Nauset Inlet. We buzzed Clifford's house, and the plane began bouncing as if in turbulence.

"What's going on?" I asked.

"Thinking about Clifford makes me twitch."

As we flew over the break at Nauset Inlet and headed north toward the wreck site, Wheeler told me about joining Clifford's treasure hunt. Wheeler thought it would be fun to get back with his college buddies. Besides, most of the pilots who flew with him in Central America were dead.

"That first season we drilled as many holes as the weather and the mailboxes allowed. We drilled from sunrise to sunset. Of course we were in the wrong area. When I came back in '85, after the wreck was found, we were always digging in places that had already been dug. It was ridiculous. I'd come up from a dive and say 'It was colder than hell and I couldn't see anything,' and then a couple of other divers would come up with coins. They were just recycling treasure. We called it *showtime*.

"My last night aboard the *Vast Explorer* I found a gold bar about so big." Wheeler put the stick between his knees and held his hands about five inches apart. "We had this swimming-pool light hanging off the back of the boat. Late at night, after the archaeologists went ashore, we could go back into the pits. I hadn't been paid in weeks. This bar was like having Bo Derek standing naked in front of you."

"What'd you do?"

"Threw it back into the ocean."

"Don't shit me."

"You've got to think of the long run. I sold my shotguns to make it through this past winter. I was starving to death. There is one thing I have learned about lying. A lie is something you have to carry with you. It's just too hard to carry lies."

We dipped low over the model of Marconi Station and turned out to sea. "We've got to get on fish," he said.

We flew for about eight hours that day and found a single school with half a dozen giant tuna. They flashed like silver and may have been worth as much, but each throw with the harpoon went wide. Afterward, everyone met at a restaurant near the dock in Barnstable. We drank a lot of beer (except Wheeler, who doesn't anymore) and left determined to succeed the next day. Wheeler went to his girlfriend's for the night, and I went to the house Wheeler rented from Rob McClung. In the hallway I pulled the trapdoor down from the ceiling, and a folding stair dropped from the attic. It was pitch black up there, but I was too impatient to find a flashlight. I crawled through a rack full of clothes and banged my head on a rafter before I felt a string hanging down. I pulled it and found myself in the middle of a stack of file boxes.

The mother lode?

McClung had been up here briefly a couple weeks before. He found samples of his maps, which he sent to me. But while those samples were more detailed than what was officially recorded in MEI's 1984 Annual Report, they weren't enough. Somewhere, said McClung, was the Master Plot of the wreck—and all its cannons. But maybe the map was lost.

Since I was going to be staying at his house, McClung finally agreed to let me look for myself. It was about two o'clock in the morning when I opened an unmarked folder and discovered a diagram of a grail found, drawn in pen and pencil by the man who first wrapped his fingers around it. Forty cannons mapped! The Master Plot!

Sure enough, the drawing depicted the same area that E.F. Hutton had raised millions to dig up: the impact zone. The mother lode. And, as McClung said, the site in '84 looked very different from the site in '87. Before Hutton raised millions for those careful measurements, MEI had blown the area to pieces.

Eureka!

McClung's drawings revealed a final mystery: the story of the *Whydah's* caboose, or stove. Back in 1850 Henry David Thoreau wrote:

> ...the violence of the seas moves the sands on the outer bar, so at times the iron caboose of the ship (that is Bellamy's) at low ebbs has been seen.

In modern times, the caboose was featured on a rough drawing by McClung dated September 21, 1984, as well as on the Master Plot. McClung told me the caboose was found in good shape under about eight feet of sand. Although the caboose was not mentioned in MEI's 1984 Annual Report, it was in the 1985 Report. Among McClung's drawings was an elegant depiction of the caboose as well as the *Whydah*'s bell. The whereabouts of the caboose was not a well kept secret, and yet on June 24, 1988—almost four years after it was discovered by divers—the caboose was discovered again for the *Cape Cod Times*:

> *Clifford Locates Whydah's 'Caboose'*
>
> South Wellfleet—Treasure-ship salvor Barry Clifford yesterday said that his crew has found the "caboose," or galley, of the pirate ship *Whydah*, an important piece of Cape Cod folklore..."
>
> He called the item "priceless..."
>
> "Certainly the caboose marked the spot where the *Whydah* was supposed to have sunk. This is the one that Thoreau talked about," Clifford said...
>
> Only about five percent of the site has been excavated, which is why, Clifford said "We're still looking for the mother lode." There's "sure to be several tons" of jewels, coins and silver remaining, he said...

I wondered why Clifford bothered to rediscover the caboose—until I remembered that E.F. Hutton's millions were raised in three installments: the first $3 million ($20,000 per unit) was due upon joining the partnership in 1987; the next $1.5 million ($10,000 per unit) was due January 15, 1988; and the final $1.5 million was due January 15, 1989. According to Hutton's prospectus, Roland Betts didn't have to raise all $6 million. If Betts felt the excavation wasn't paying off, he could have stopped at $3 million or at $4.5 million. To keep Hutton's money flowing, Clifford had to keep making discoveries...

This was just a theory of course. And yet, on October 12, 1989, Roland Betts wrote to his investors:

> An attempt was also made to recover the ship's stove, an artifact that was discovered and tagged during the 1988 field season. Unfortunately, once again the elements did not cooperate. Maritime found an additional 2-3 feet of sand covering the site, which created a 15-20 foot overburden. Attempts to raise the stove threatened to destroy the artifact. Consequently, it was decided to leave the stove in place and monitor the sand level for possible excavation next summer.

The "priceless" caboose is still loose. After so many discoveries, it has been blown too deep and is too badly damaged to be recovered.

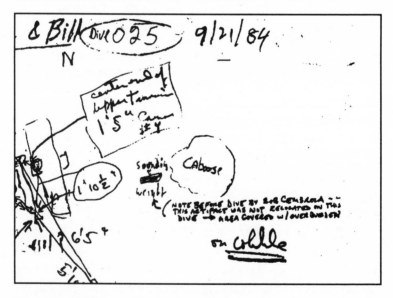

Though not discovered for the newspapers or Hutton's investors until 1988, the *Whydah's* stove, or "caboose," was first drawn by Rob McClung on September 21, 1984.

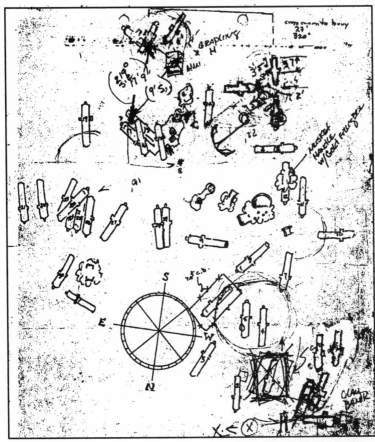

In 1984, Aspen's former police chief, Rob McClung, compiled this Master Plot locating about 40 buried cannons on the *Whydah* site. This map is significant because the *Whydah* was previously thought to have carried only 28 guns (the additional guns may have been stored in the hold and some may have been counted twice) and because the first salvor wrote in 1717: "The Riches with the Guns will be Buried in the Sand."

In other words, this is a map of the *Whydah*'s mother lode.

In 1987, E.F. Hutton raised $6 million for an archaeological excavation of this same area. Oddly enough, this rough map may be more accurate than the maps created with Hutton's millions. Before the archaeologists took over, the site was blown to pieces.

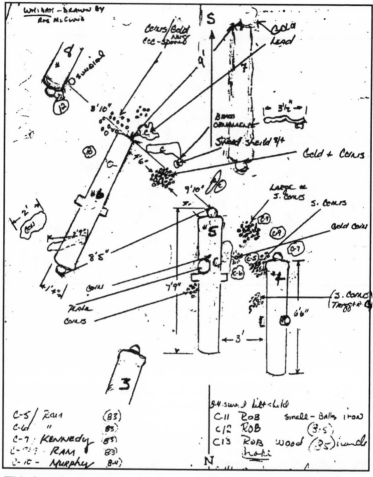

This drawing is a detail of six cannons (#3-#8) presumably discovered
on August 3-4, 1984, by divers McClung, Murphy, and Kennedy. It
is one of several details that McClung used to create his Master Plot.

Barry Clifford would tell the press and investors that only two
pits were dug in 1984, and that all the treasure that was brought up
had been tightly packed in a tiny area (3,000 coins in a single 8-inch-
by-8-inch test pit). But this drawing shows otherwise. The coins were
evenly distributed. Looking at this drawing and the Master Plot, a
potential investor might have thought twice.

But investors were not shown these details.

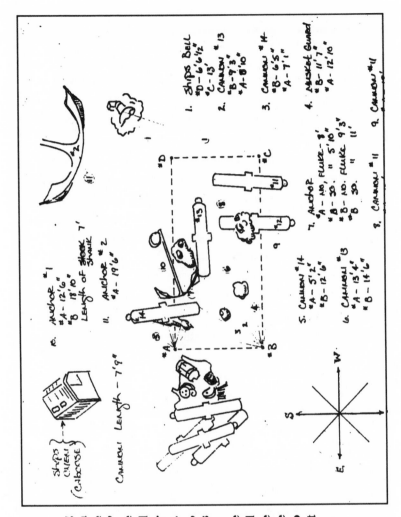

In 1985, McClung drew this map locating a bell, inscribed "The Whydah Gally 1716" (Upper right below the large anchor). The bell was about the last major artifact found on the site. For the Wall Streeters, however, the bell rang as a call to investors.

Note the caboose (upper left), which would be "discovered" three years later to encourage E.F. Hutton's investors to pay the final installment of $1.5 million.

On Tuesday morning, September 11, 1990, I was at my desk fussing over the final draft of "Dogfights Over Fish" for *Sports Illustrated* when the buzzer rang from the lobby. I was expecting my mother-in-law, but it proved to be a man with legal papers. "Who are they from?" I asked through the intercom. He read from the return address the name of the famous First Amendment law firm.

What now? I wondered.

I'd heard through the grapevine that the book packager had hired a new writer, a novelist, to write *The Pirate Prince*. Hiring a novelist to ghostwrite for Clifford seemed brilliant: it would provide deniability for everyone. Meanwhile, I was muzzled by the original contract, and McClung's Master Plot was tucked away in my safe-deposit box.

But Lief didn't know I had the Master Plot. Maybe he never believed me? Maybe he'd really blown it?

I rode the elevator down to the lobby and found a young man outside the iron gate. He looked relieved to see me. "I really appreciate you coming down," he said. "I hate to do this." He handed me a summons from the civil court of the City of New York.

I leaned against the gate and read the four short paragraphs charging me with having "failed to write and deliver the agreed text " and demanding $25,000 with interest from the day I was fired.

"You okay?" The young man asked.

"Sure," I muttered. "I'm dealing with dopes."

He looked startled.

"*With* dopes."

I went back upstairs and called a lawyer (the second firm on the list McGrath had given me). I had met with the lawyer once and had shown him both the maps and Hutton's prospectus. Now I read him the complaint.

"I'm very surprised," he said. "Baffled." He paused. "I guess the real question is, who's behind this?"

"I would guess it's not just Lief, but I don't know. What'll it cost me to find out?"

"We'll need a retainer of ten thousand dollars to deal with the complaint. If it goes to court, it might be fifty thousand."

I now understood the gambit. *Sports Illustrated* was paying $1,250 for the tuna piece.

The lawyer read my silence for what it was. "Of course you could probably settle for ten grand. If you promise never to write about it, they might drop the whole thing."

"Maybe I should offer to sell them the maps."

"Blackmail? Our firm doesn't do that."

"Unfortunately, neither does mine. Let me call you back."

I called my mother. "What do I do?"

"I'll send you a check."

Thanks, Mom.

For the next couple of weeks I spent a lot of time wondering whether Betts was behind the lawsuit—and thinking about what he had become. When Hutton's offering closed, Betts had achieved every boy's dream. He controlled a real pirate treasure in gold and silver, as well as millions in cash. He had a huge ship with a black flag on the masthead. His gala launching the adventure got featured on the *Today Show*, with his investors dressed up as pirates.

But the same morning that *Today* broadcast Betts' gala from New York, his flagship blew up in Louisiana. And then it reached the Cape and almost ran aground.

Betts must have sensed then that he had swallowed a hook...

And then Clifford began hauling in the line.

A big yank came in MEI's '87 Annual Report, a thick document done with all the minutia a multimillion-dollar investment can provide. Page 66 had a detail not mentioned in previous reports or in Hutton's prospectus:

> In addition to the 28 cannons which were reported to have been mounted on deck; it is believed that she carried at least a dozen more cannons in her hold, since Director of Operations Rob McClung obtained a rough tally of 44 cannons during the course of the survey in the 1984 season.

Another yank came in a videotaped lab tour led by the piratologist Ken Kinkor. The tour opened with a credit to MEI and then E.F. Hutton's black flag. According to the piratologist, MEI's divers had "tagged more than 40 cannons."

And so, by the fall of 1987, Betts should have known that Clifford's divers had located all the cannons. And surely Betts was familiar with Southack's quote—the one Clifford recited to Cronkite on prime time: *"The Riches with the Guns will be Buried in the Sand."*

One can imagine Clifford laughing at him: "We're not *playing* pirates. We *are* pirates. We've got to sail to the Azores." But in the meantime, the stock market crashed, and the Golden Age of Corporate Raiders began to smell like rotten fish.

By January 1988, Betts faced a major decision: whether to collect the second installment from Hutton's investors. Collecting the money would increase their risk. Not collecting it would admit defeat.

Betts collected the money.

Of course, Betts may have still believed in a fabulous mother lode. And yet, only days after the installment was due, he accepted an offer from a company called History, Inc., to buy out the Hutton partnership for about $3.6 million, plus

$900,000 for Konkapot's stock options in MEI. The deal would have allowed Hutton's investors a small profit. Unfortunately, History, Inc., was none other than Bruce Heafitz—who couldn't come up with the money because Clifford had already fleeced him.

The next year, Betts had to decide whether to collect the final installment from his investors. Maybe he really believed that the caboose had just been discovered—and that there were more discoveries to come. Or maybe he was just too badly hooked to fight back. Whatever the reason, he called in the money, most of which would be spent on artifact conservation. To finance the final dive season, Betts sold his investors' interest in the great flagship to Heafitz—a sale that ultimately garnered three pieces of silver and a booger of gold.

Meanwhile, on September 24, 1990, Rob McClung called me from the Empire Hotel on Broadway at West 63rd Street, and we agreed to meet for breakfast. I was worried. McClung's Master Plot implicated him as well as Clifford. But when I placed a copy of the map on the breakfast table, McClung went over it in detail and agreed to testify on my behalf. Some people might have paid a lot for that map, but McClung didn't demand a dime—nor did he dictate how it should be used.

McClung also explained what happened to him in Aspen. Chief McClung didn't steal a .357 magnum and give it to Judge Levin. McClung gave his own service revolver, another .357, to the judge.

And McClung had a reason for stashing the missing .357 in his desk. It happened during a routine inventory of the property locker. His officers had spread guns all over the office, and the chief wanted to test their security precautions. None of the guns in the property locker were evidence in criminal cases. McClung took one, and nobody noticed. Unfortunately, the chief also forgot about the gun until the owner came.

McClung told the truth about what had happened—but his plan to reprimand his officers backfired. Then the press got hold of the story. The local reporters didn't believe McClung—and didn't appreciate his drug arrests—so they took the opportunity to crucify him.

I asked McClung why he didn't stay in Aspen to fight the charges, and the former police chief recoiled as if in pain.

"There never were any charges!"

He collected himself and continued. "As police chief I had responsibility for the gun, and it was in my desk. Nothing was stolen. I wasn't worried about charges."

"Then why did you resign?"

McClung sat back and sighed. "I had been away in Europe for the Police Ski Team World Championships, and I walked into the city manager's office thinking the gun case was no big deal. I didn't understand how much the story had grown until the city manager said he was going to have to suspend me without pay while the thing was investigated. Maybe six months. I couldn't hold out that long. All my money was in a new $350,000 house on the golf course. I couldn't afford that anyway.

"I didn't cut a deal to avoid prosecution, if that's what you're thinking," McClung continued. "I challenged the D.A. to charge me with something. *Anything.* And he said he was not pursuing it. If he had charged me, I would have stayed. But he didn't, so I resigned... I had to."

McClung went on with his story as we ate breakfast, but I didn't understand what he meant until much later when we were friends. McClung had played the game fast and loose in Aspen: free skis from K-2; a fling with a movie star; and finally a real incident with a pistol. It took place in that new house on the golf course—with one of his own officers.

McClung realized then that he had to start over. Somehow, he had created his own predicament for "intuitive reasons."

McClung lost his wife. He lost his house. He lost his career. He sold his possessions and poured his father's ashes over the Continental Divide on his way to join his best friend on a treasure hunt. McClung thought they had a deal, but when he got to the Cape he had been cut out. There was no room for him in the Captain's house. He was put in the crew's quarters with a pittance for stock and no income. McClung discovered the wreck and did his best with it. And he swore he would pay them back in spades.

Before we parted, McClung wrote the following on the back of the Master Plot:

> "I drew this map of the *Whydah* site before [Warren Riess' archaeological team] arrived July/ August 1984.
>
> > (Signed) Rob McClung

I made a copy, had it framed, and hung it on my wall for luck.

On October 19, I matched the book packager's $25,000 lawsuit and raised him $1 million in punitive damages related to the stock offering. Soon afterward, we agreed on a settlement. I would pay back almost all of what I had received, and he would rip up the original contract—leaving me free to publish a true account of what had happened. It seemed the honorable course, and I must have figured that I would make a lot of money from the book, because I took my wife to Petrossian for her birthday. Smoked trout, three kinds of caviar, two bottles of champagne and a birthday cake plus tax and tip came to more than $600. The maitre d' shook my hand, and my wife and I stepped out into the lights of the big city.

Epilogue

Ideas came flying into my head today. It's been
foggy for awhile. But it has cleared. The deal is no
longer a speculative one. We can build a museum,
lab, ect. My promise can be kept. With a museum I
could influence thousands of children. I promise that
will be my major goal—if I am allowed to succeed.

—The log of Barry Clifford,
September 19, 1983

It was Sunday, January 6, 1991, the Feast of the Epiphany,
and I was in the Episcopal Church of the Epiphany in Providence, Rhode Island, fidgeting in my pew so noticeably that
an elderly woman leaned over and whispered kindly, "Are
you having trouble?" Startled, I smiled and tried to get back
in step with the choreography. This was a small but obviously devout group of worshipers. They sang with their hearts
and didn't glance at their watches.

I hadn't been to church in years, but the Rector, Fred Brunson, was a close friend. I had called him to say I needed a place to stay, and he offered me the spare rooms upstairs in the rectory. Separating for a few weeks was my wife's idea, and I was angry and lost. She expected me to go home to California, but as I packed my clothes and my office, I pictured Father Fred in his chair, smoke trickling languidly upward from his pipe, wearing an expression of rapture that made the Buddha look like an options trader. All I wanted in the world was one of his pipes. So I drove to Providence, and he picked one out for me. We drank scotch, listened to "Jerusalem," smoked our pipes, and talked long into the night. He said that I was not the man he once saw on the *Today Show* and invited to talk to his congregation about the pursuit of excellence.

Now, listening to him preach, I had to admit that he was right.

The eighties had unraveled for me a couple of weeks earlier at Beth Israel Hospital, where I had helped transfer my friend Tim from the medical ward to the psychiatric ward. The police had been summoned. His doctor wanted him in handcuffs. His sisters huddled in the hallway keeping out of his sight because their presence set him off. But I was an old friend and calmed him enough for the journey.

A day or so later I was on the phone with Maya Lin, the architect, when he phoned her from the ward. He wanted us to come quickly and to bring pens and paper. When we arrived he was lying down. His eyes were wide and blank and deep. His voice was almost toneless, as if coming from somewhere far away. His speech was repetitive—sometimes very fast and incoherent. He said he was very tired, that he had a lot he needed to say and not much time. He took our hands and made us swear to go out and tell the truth. Awkwardly, bashfully, in front of one another, we said we would. But he didn't tell us what it was.

It was no mystery why he went mad. There was the new stress of an architecture project in Japan, the continuing stress of trying to protect his family from bad news, and then the allergic reaction to an experimental drug, a reaction that marked his transition from HIV-positive to AIDS. As his temperature climbed beyond 105 degrees, he snapped.

It was also no mystery why he phoned Maya. She was about 20 years old when she wrote the only completely true statement about the war in Viet Nam. She did the same for those nine who gave their lives for civil rights, and perhaps she will be called upon to do the same for the millions who will die of AIDS.

But why me? It was not of such consequence, but I wrote the reason in *The Shell Game*—a race on a cold and windy day at Nottingham, England, in the summer of 1979.

> Huddled against the wind, I thought of my sweat shirt lying warm and dry on the dock. I had anticipated a quick race... Wearing only a wet T-shirt and shorts, I soon began to shake uncontrollably. After about twenty minutes Tony, who had been riding alongside the course on a bicycle, noticed that I looked very cold and lent me his jacket from the 1968 Olympic games. I wore it until we went to the line and then wrapped it around my feet. I considered leaving it on, but I couldn't. I had not earned the right to wear such a jacket in the first place. I certainly could not race in it...
>
> In every race there was a conscious decision to pull to win or perhaps not to. At any moment it seemed that the boat would decide that losing was not that painful. I was cold and sick of racing. The conditions were so blatantly unfair that rowing hardly seemed worthwhile. Cal had disappeared.

With a straight start in much flatter water, they
moved ahead by two lengths in the first two hundred
meters. Czechoslovakia was only a little ahead but
they were a national team. The Bulgarians had won
last year, the Russians a few years before that. Yale
did not fit the list.

A wave broke over the gunwale, dousing my
shorts as the bow swung back around. The sudden
chill riveted my eyes downward, focusing them on
the USA jacket at my feet. I wanted one of those
jackets. It seemed to me bad enough that I had worn
the jacket without earning it, but it felt reprehensible
to put it on and then lose heart. Angrily and with a
trace of fear, I began to pull...

Desperately we cranked up the stroke rating to
38. With twenty strokes to go, Andy called the rating
up two more strokes. Ten strokes later he called it
up two more. The rhythm was breaking. Last five!
"Easy!" The Czechs finished less than a second
behind, wondering how a university could beat a
national team.

I believed then that truth and strength were the same and
made the Olympic team. I believed the Olympics were sa-
cred—part of a inviolable code of honor.

And then there was the boycott.

Sure, we got jackets with the five rings and even gold
medals on the steps of the Capitol. President Carter showed
up to tell us what a great day he was having: something like:
"Why just this morning I met Miss America and Miss Universe in the Oval Office, and now I'm meeting the United
States Olympic team." Most of the rowers stood there with
hands in pockets looking at the President as if he were a bad
piece of cheese. But I shook hands with him and gave him a
pin with the five rings. He cut my heart out, and I gave him
the pin. Why? I voted for him in November to prove I wasn't
sore, and never voted again. I went to Ireland hoping to write

a novel. I stood on the edge of a raw promontory jutting out over the boiling Atlantic, wondering if I should hurl myself in. Instead, I sank into a sea of self-pity and rage.

The Shell Game came out tough as nails. In another five minutes on the *Today Show,* I could have nailed Jane Pauley. My snarling photo was in *Andy Warhol's Interview*, and then the head of ABC's casting department tracked me down to screen test for Adam Carrington on *Dynasty*. I could do anything. On a whim I asked Sigourney Weaver to dinner, and she accepted. I set out to make the '84 Olympic team on an hour a day to prove it wasn't worth a full-time effort. I wrote a long feature for *The New Yorker* about a mutiny on the Oxford crew, exposing the corruption of the oldest amateur tradition in the world. I rowed the hardest races of my life for a Gillette commercial. I bought a motorboat. And I got hooked by the son of some unknown swindler out fishing. He reeled me in and came at me with his knife, and I didn't flinch because I had gutted myself already. I had become a hollow space surrounded by crusty iron emitting a gradually diminishing magnetic field.

Communion was starting. Rather than make a spectacle I joined the line, accepted the host, and felt, for the moment, that I belonged. When the service was over, and the last of the candles extinguished, I walked toward the door feeling comfortable for the first time in months. A guest book was on the table near the exit, and so I paused to write my name and address in the appropriate columns. At the right of the address column was a third blank I hadn't reckoned on—a space that filled me with panic. Everyone else had filled it in with an appropriate response. For a moment I considered inventing something, but I left it empty.

The blank was for "Home Church."

Epilogue

A man without a home church seems a definition of a journalist. Not a confidence man. Rather, a person stumbling forward—sometimes to dangerous, ruinous, and morally indefensible extremes—propelled by a supreme lack of confidence. My only redemption would be to strive to find and record truths that people cry for in times of madness. Such was my epiphany on the Feast of the Epiphany in the Church of the Epiphany in Providence.

When symbols bash you on the head, you go with it.

I resolved then to finish my book before I returned home, and I worked feverishly on a diet of scotch and gin. One night I woke up terrified and drenched in sweat to find my room in the rectory glowing bright white. Six inches of new snow had fallen, and the glow was the reflection of halogen security lights through the dormer windows. I staggered to the dormer and stood looking outward, shivering with dread and clinging to the frame—my view filled with the wooden church draped in snow against the blackness of the city. I felt the presence of evil. I could sense it all around me, dancing in the periphery of my vision. So long as I kept my eyes focused on the brightness in front of me, the evil was impotent. I knew for the first time in my life that there is a God.

I returned to Manhattan on February 4 with a draft of what I hoped was *New Yorker*-caliber journalism. Jennifer wasn't home. She had insisted that our reunion take place at the therapist's office, and I wrote back that I would meet her anywhere on the planet but there. I was never going back there. But I also told her I would return on a Tuesday, and I didn't. The book wasn't done. I came home on Wednesday.

On Thursday, when she came home, we talked for hours. I had resolved to be completely open about anything and everything. She took notes, and I found her more paper when she ran out. We didn't talk at any length again until Valentine's Day. I gave her a sculpture holding a rose, and she gave me the card of her attorney.

"Why?"

"Don't give me that bullshit. It's what you said. It's in my notes."

She also said she had taken the Jeep and had cashed out the $50,000 remaining in our home equity credit line. As she left, she said her mother was frantic about my Mercedes. I called my mother-in-law, got a ride out to Darien, and sold the car for what you can get when you're desperate and will take nothing but cash. When I returned to Manhattan, the elevator opened into an empty hallway. The dining table was still in the dining room, the breakables were still in the cabinets, and my office was intact. Otherwise, the place was empty.

The final pieces of that particular puzzle, which were relayed through the attorneys, was my decision to stay with a priest and my letter declaring that I would never return to Peter's office. Peter and Linda had read my letter and said it was a smokescreen. And everybody knows that priests are gay. It's all you read in the papers.

And though none of it was true, the end was appropriate. Shoot marbles for your marriage, and you'll be wiped out.

Looking back at that time, what surprised me most is that Tim made it out of the psych ward. He really liked being waited on. He had a nice view. They fed him regularly. And given what he had to look forward too, I figured he would choose not to get better. But his family rallied in the most remarkable way, and so did he. Even before the doctors would let him go, his architecture studio had moved into the ward. As soon as he got out, he flew to Japan to present the design, and they didn't notice that he was mad. Perhaps they thought all Americans are that way.

Meanwhile, I borrowed money from my mother to pay the settlement with Lief, and then my agent sent the manuscript out. Chip McGrath said he was impressed. It wasn't a *New Yorker* story, he said, but it was a good book. The book publishers, however, sent it back. So did magazines. I revised it, still as a piece of journalism, got more rejections, and went kind of nuts.

Then a friend faxed me an editorial by the editor of *Forbes:*

Litigation and the First Amendment

New Yorker Roland Betts, a former entertainment lawyer, has made a ton of money from the movies, big money, many millions of dollars. Betts doesn't make movies or show them. He has offered ordinary investors a shot at financing them.... Investors haven't made big money from the deals. Betts has.

But he can't stand criticism. So it was when Forbes looked at his Silver Screen Partners IV and found it wanting as an investment, Betts sued us for a whole laundry list of things: libel, injurious falsehood, blah, blah, blah. Betts didn't have much of a case, but it didn't stop him. Perhaps he was determined to punish us and discourage others in the media from commenting unfavorably on his merchandise. For three years the case dragged on with lengthy pretrial proceedings. Meanwhile, he admitted in a report to his investors that Silver Screen Partners IV had "disappointing" results from its films.

Last month the New York State Supreme Court Justice Shirley Fingerhood threw Betts' case out of court, granting Forbes summary judgment and ruling that our story was accurate in fact and fair in its opinions. Defending the case has cost Forbes lots of money and has taken lots of time editors, reporters, and executives could have spent more

> productively—a sad waste. Yet it is part of the cost
> in these litigious times of doing what Forbes does:
> first finding and weighing the facts; then drawing
> strong, unhedged conclusions from them. That's
> what our readers pay us for, and the Roland Bettses
> of this world cannot shut us up.

As admirable as those sentiments were, *Forbes* didn't publish the original piece with the expectation of spending three years in court. And, after *Forbes'* experience, no publisher could be expected to touch *Walking the Plank*—whether or not it was true.

Yet the game went on.

The novelist who replaced me on *The Pirate Prince* finished a draft—some 85,000 words—but Lief demanded revisions. The account of Bernstein and Betts' involvement with marketing the pirate story was deleted. Then the entire manuscript was unacceptable. The writer kept his $10,000 advance but was not paid the remainder of the contract. A manuscript doctor took on *The Pirate Prince*.

Then another.

Then another.

I don't know how many ghosts and doctors danced around the book, but in April 1993 *Reader's Digest* published a condensed version. In June *The Pirate Prince: Discovering the Priceless Treasure of the Sunken Ship Whydah* emerged from Simon & Schuster, which had devoured Prentice Hall. Clifford dedicated it:

> *To my brave and loyal brethren*
> *who ventured out with me*
> *to where the Earth dropped off*
> *and found the greatest treasure of all:*
> *true friendship*

Epilogue

Contrary to what he swore to the court in Massachusetts, Clifford admitted in *The Pirate Prince* that Matt Costa wasn't packing a pistol. Despite what he told E.F. Hutton for their prospectus, Clifford admitted his blunder with the *General Arnold*. Clifford even mentioned the barnacles—and that the wreck must have been exposed from time to time.

Those truths came out, I suppose, because otherwise Clifford would have been lying. Or maybe it was simply because my agent had sent *Walking the Plank* to Simon & Schuster.

The Pirate Prince went on to describe how Clifford felt when it came time to present the *Whydah* offering to the E.F. Hutton brokers in Denver. Clifford was sweating, talking aloud to himself:

> "Why aren't we rich?"
>
> "What?" Rob McClung said.
>
> "That's what they're going to say. 'If you're sitting on all this pirate treasure, why aren't you rich?'"
>
> "These guys know the business," Rob said. "They understand about development money and overhead."
>
> "This is crazy. Would Sam Bellamy have done this? Can you see him typing annual reports? 'This season featured over fifty hostile mergers, leading to the acquisition of thirty—'"
>
> "Barry, we're not pirates."

According to McClung, Clifford wasn't in Denver when the deal was presented to E.F. Hutton. Bernstein and Betts didn't catch the mistake. From reading *The Pirate Prince,* you'd never know it was theirs.

And still the game goes on! Now in the selfless colors of the nineties.

After finding the *Whydah*, it was my dream to establish a museum... The urge for freedom is a desire we need to nurture, the sorts of conditions that drove pirates to murder and steal in the name of freedom still need to be fought... Perhaps never before has a time capsule come to us at a more critical moment.

I tried to pursue leads quietly; by this time investors were asking when we were going to start selling all that gold and silver, all those priceless guns and pewter plates. Word got back to Bernstein and Betts—

—and they were all for it.

After long negotiations, plans were created for a museum, featuring a full scale re-creation of the ship—complete with a simulation of the fatal storm, a working conservation laboratory—tons of concretions, doubtlessly holding untold treasures, will be opened right before the public's eye... and, of course the artifacts.

The bottom line: The museum would cost $70 million.

I used to think $250,000 was a lot. Roland and Tom assured me that the museum could be financed and running by 1995...

Understand this, the mother lode is still out there... Somewhere there are tons of cannon balls, cannons, swivel guns, and the treasure they stored with it... Southack knew it. He said, "The riches with the guns will be buried in the sand."

And I...

I sat in a hospital and watched my friend die inch by inch, then packed up my belongings, and bailed out of New York City. I drove to Oregon, bought a new white-water kayak, and finally learned to roll in rapids. I fell in love with a woman who knows how to row, and now there's a child on the way. I tried to get on with new projects. But I was stuck writing in the first person, in real time. With every word my puzzle changed shape, and already it was much too large and too unstable not to lock in some final piece. I had made a promise. I had to cast myself. Who am I? What am I? A sucker? A loser? A liar? A coward? I thought of my jacket with the five rings. All I wanted was to wear it honestly again, with pride. I drew myself up in front of my word processor and recited from the words of Daniel Defoe:

> I am a freelancer, and I have as much right to engage the whole world as he who has an army of 100,000 attorneys in the field: and this my conscience tells me. And I will fight with snively nosed Yale brats, or anyone else who kicks people about deck with pleasure, and destroys the faith of those who practice and believe in what they preach.

It felt good so I said it again. And again. And again.

After all, there's a sizable army of us: freelance writers, editors, fact checkers, designers, printers, binders, publicists, and independent booksellers. All we need to do is sail within range of their big cannons and dance. At some point they won't be able to take it. They'll have to reach for the linstock, touch the flaming wad to the touch-hole. Chances are nothing at all will happen. But perhaps Clifford wasn't lying: that saturated gunpowder still packs a punch, and the big guns will explode in a cataclysm of barnacles.

At least I hope so.

Acknowledgements

A man alone ain't got no bloody chance.
— Earnest Hemingway

It is a few months short of five years since my first meeting with Barry Clifford, *Walking The Plank* is finally shipping off to the printer, and I am making reservations to return to Cape Cod. Whatever happens there, I would like to thank those who have helped along the way. I alone bear responsibility for what is written here, but without your encouragement I wouldn't have made it.

Amy C. Cuddy, Nancy Hunt Kiesling, Roy Kiesling II, Jennie Kiesling, Brady Kiesling, Roy Kiesling III, Janet Hutchison, Fred Brunson, Roger Kennedy, Eric Ashworth, Edward Hibbert, Barbara Kevles, Matthew & Catharine Labine, Anne Larrivee, Charles Kaiser, T George Harris, Joe Sprung, Charles McGrath, Alvin Deutsch, Fred Greenman, Kevin Smith, Deirdre O'Farrelly, Beth Lenahan, Jenny Longly, Maya Lin, David Potter, John Biglow, Seth Bauer, Pat Smith, Senter Jones, Fontaine Syer, John Cole, the Seltzers, Linda Alper, and especially Kevin Cooney, who said, "You gotta make it sleazier."

I would also like to thank all of the people involved with the *Whydah* who were willing to talk frankly about what happened. In particular, I would like to thank Robert Reedy, Todd Murphy, Charles Burnham, William Crockett, Bruce Heafitz, Mel Fisher, Fay Feild, Matt Costa, Warren Riess, Edwin Dethlefsen, Trip Wheeler, and especially Robert McClung, a fine man and a great treasure hunter. I would also like to thank Paul Johnston, J. Barto Arnold, and Seth Rolbein for their special insights into the story.

Finaly, I would like to give special thanks to Cathy Coombs for the first cover concept; Susan Welt, who made it work; Alexis Lipsitz for copy editing; Micheal McRae for my photograph; Sheila Drescher and Nancy Peterson at Bloomsbury Books in Ashland for their encouragement; and to Laura Young, who has been an invaluable editor, organizer, and friend during the launch of Nordic Knight.

STEPHEN KIESLING was born in Texas, in 1958, and grew up in Palo Alto, California. He was educated at Yale, where he was a Scholar of the House in philosophy and a member of the 1980 U.S. Olympic Rowing Team. He spent the eighties in Manhattan, where he helped launch *American Health* magazine and Nike's Cross-Training program. He has written for *The New Yorker*, *Sports Illustrated*, and *Outside*, and edited for the *Harvard Business Review*. He now lives in Ashland, Oregon.

(photo by Michael McRae)